Yo-Yo Tricks: From Beginner to Spinner

Prima's Yo-Yo Book

Mario De Govia
Joe Arnold
Thaddaeus D. Winzenz

Prima Games
A Division of Prima Communications, Inc.

3875 Atherton Road
Rocklin, CA 95765
(916) 632-4400
www.primagames.com

Project Editor: David Mathews
Product Manager: Sara E. Wilson
Photography: Danny DeFoe
Photos in the Yo-Yo Competitions Chapter courtesy of Fiend Magazine

Team Bird Members:
Angelo Hatcher
Julian Hennebery
Sam Miller
Hieu Ngo
Kevin Scott
Matthew Siameng
Julian Tran
Alex Aguilera

Special thanks to Bob Malowney

Library of Congress Catalog Card Number: 99-62824
Printed in the United States of America

99 00 01 02 KK 10 9 8 7 6 5 4 3 2 1

Table of Contents

Yo-Yo Intro

Hello!

Looking to learn how to use that shiny new yo-yo? Want to figure out how to do the more advanced tricks all your friends know and won't teach you?

Then this, friends, is the book for you.

We—that is, Joe, Thaddaeus, and Mario—will take you through the world of "spinning" step by step.

With a little help from our friends.

With Danny DeFoe's talented camera-work, we're able to show you real people doing the tricks. The photos you see in this book are of hard-working members of Team Bird, the competitive yo-yo team based out of the Bird in Hand store in Chico, California. Each of the models you see can do the tricks they're demonstrating—plus a whole lot more!

So grab your yo-yo, warm up your arm, and get ready to yo like you've never yo'd before!

How to Use This Guide

The tricks and tips in this guide, although not guaranteed to make you a Master Class yo-er, can improve your technique and teach you an excellent range of impressive tricks. To help you learn, we've done a few things to make the organization of this guide as easy to follow as possible.

First of all, we've created icons for all the Building Block techniques and tricks. When a trick we're discussing uses Building Blocks, you'll see the pictures of all the Building Blocks you need to know to perform the trick.

Also, we've provided pictures of the important parts of each and every trick. Need to know where your hand goes? Not sure which finger goes where? Just look at the pictures for help.

With steady practice following the descriptions you read here, you'll soon be making your yo-yo do things that you didn't know were possible.

How to Read the Icons

Building Block(s) — Trick Name — Trick Icon

Basic Front Mount

Choose Your Weapon

The Rule of 5

One yo-yo is never enough!

One yo-yo is not enough for the serious spinner. Eventually, you should have at least five yo-yos in your arsenal. First, you're going to need a good looping yo-yo (two if you're going to be doing two-handed tricks), a good string-trick yo-yo, a long sleeper, a good all-purpose yo-yo... The list goes on.

All yo-yo players have different things they like about different yo-yos. Some like nylon transaxles, while others prefer ball-bearing or wood models. But all agree that you've got to try a bunch before you can decide what you like. It's even OK to switch yo-yos simply because you're bored with the one you've been using.

Try all of them out! It never hurts to practice with different kinds of yo-yos. In fact, if you can do a trick with your "worst" yo-yo, chances are you can do it with any yo-yo.

Nuts and Bolts

Here's some information on the basic types of yo-yos you can find in stores. It's always a good idea to be well informed before you pay out your cash.

Check out www.YoForIt.com to learn more about each brand before you buy.

Fixed-Axle Wooden Yo-Yos

Wooden Yo-Yo

Back in the old days, wooden yo-yos were the only yo-yos. Since then, the wooden yo-yo's simple design has become the model for the modern yo-yo.

The fixed axle of the wooden yo-yo continues to undergo constant transformation. Newer yo-yo models sport replaceable cores and take-apart halves. These features add much to their maintainability. As for the wooden yo-yo, these puppies aren't antiquated yet. Some dedicated players still love the feel and play of fixed wooden axles. One of the reasons is that wooden yo-yo's are great for looping tricks. Keep in mind though, that a wooden yo-yo doesn't sleep as long. So, when you master a complex string trick while using one, you earn the respect of your friends.

Plastic-Core Transaxle

TIP Wooden yo-yo's have a tendency to become unbalanced. To combat this, plastic yo-yos with wooden axles are available that give you the same feel on the string without the balancing problems.

Yomega FireBall™, one of many plastic transaxles on the market.

This should be the second yo-yo you get your hands on. A great all-purpose yo-yo, these babies pack a punch when it comes to sleeping and looping. If you need a more advanced yo-yo than the one you picked up for a buck at the drug store and you lack the cash for one of the fancy ball-bearing types, a plastic transaxle will do the trick.

Time for a few terms.

The axle of a yo-yo is the rod that connects the two halves together. Sometimes, as in fixed-axle yo-yos, the string rests directly on this axle.

Transaxle yo-yos have a ring of plastic or metal that goes over the axle rod. The string loops around this ring. That way, there is less friction from the string rubbing against the axle rod. In fact, the string never touches the axle rod in a transaxle yo-yo!

Here's an axle rod.

And here's the transaxle ring.

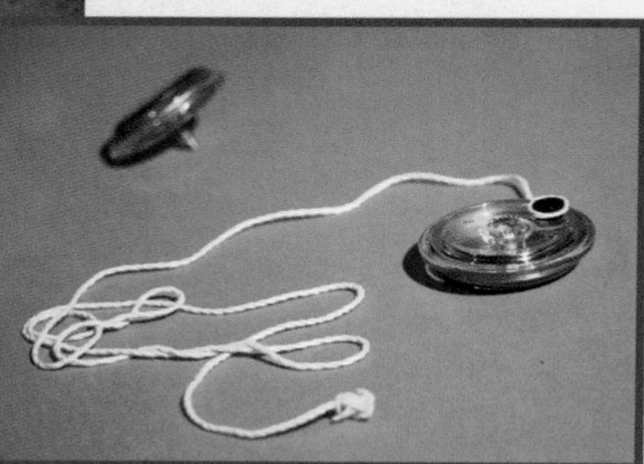

Transaxle triple looped.

String 'em Up

For *most* plastic-core transaxle yo-yos, be sure to triple loop the string around the transaxle. Because the spinning occurs between the transaxle and the axle, the string needs to latch onto the transaxle. Check the "Care and Feeding" section to learn how to attach the string.

Check the instruction manual for the manufacturer's recommendation. Regardless of what the manual says, though, try experimenting with double, triple, and even quadruple looping. Stick with what works best for you.

Trivi-Yo

Yo-yo's were popular in Greece around 500 B.C.!

Centrifugal Clutch Yo-Yos

This is a more complicated version of the regular plastic transaxle. If you're just starting down the path of yo-yo play, the best yo-yo to get would be a centrifugal-clutch yo-yo. The most popular version of this yo-yo is the Yomega Brain® Yo-Yo.

Yomega Brain®

The sweet thing about these guys is the automatic return. You'll appreciate this feature when you are just starting out. But beware—when you attempt more difficult tricks, the yo-yo will try to climb back up the string when you least expect it.

Guts of a Yomega Brain®

NOTE Notice that the axle can't move when it's still? This makes the string easy to wind, but here's what is really happening. Springs hold stoppers against the transaxle part of the yo-yo. When the yo-yo spins, the centrifugal force releases the stoppers—allowing the yo-yo to sleep. When the spin slows down, the centrifugal force can no longer hold back the spring. This causes the stoppers to engage the transaxle, forcing the yo-yo to wind back up the string.

Ball-Bearing Transaxle

If you can toss a screamin' Sleeper and do a few string tricks with your plastic-core transaxle, it's time to save up for a ball-bearing transaxle yo-yo.

The inside of a Team Losi Da Bomb®

They're worth it.

We prefer this style of yo-yo to all others. Although some ball-bearing yo-yos don't loop as well as others, they sleep forever. These yo-yos allow plenty of time for those complex string tricks.

The ball-bearing yo-yos add another level of friction reduction. They have the regular axle rod, but their transaxle ring is different. There's the inner ring and the outer ring. In between the two are little ball bearings. The effect is a really, really long Sleeper.

Shapes

The different shapes of the yo-yos out there all have a purpose. What purpose? Read on...

Koosh™ ProYo II®

Traditional

This is the most versatile shape for a yo-yo. These yo-yos are especially good for Looping tricks, but you can use them for string tricks as well.

Wing and Butterfly

This shape isn't good for Looping, but it's a sweet design for string tricks. A yo-yo like this will make your life a whole lot easier when you're learning Man on the Flying Trapeze.

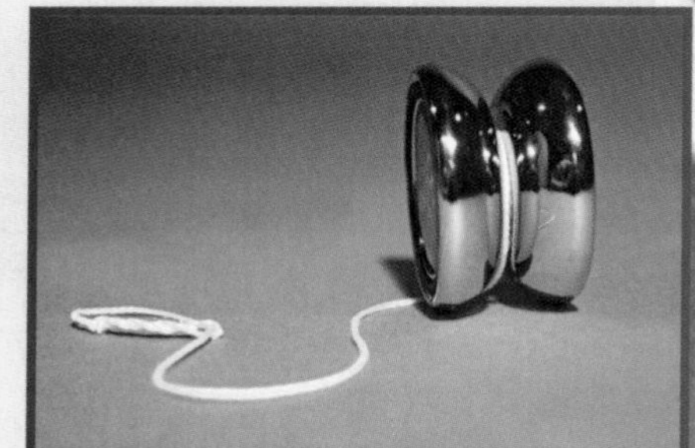

Team Losi Silver Series Butterfly Design

Materials

Plastic

Made of a space-age polymer, these yo-yos are designed with your hands in mind. Plastic yo-yos are your friends. They are light, long lasting, withstand abuse, and don't hurt (as much) when they fall on your head.

A Yomega Saber Raider™

Tom Kuhn's Silver Bullet 2®

Metal

Precision engineering and insane sleeping times both characterize metal yo-yos. If you ever need to go for that 1-minute Sleeper or need to do multiple string tricks in a row, you must get your hands on one of these.

They are *expensive*. They are *heavy*. They are *cool*. You don't need one right away; make sure you're serious before you snap one up.

So What Do I Buy?

Start with a solid, beginner's yo-yo like the Yomega FireBall™, or a Duncan™ if you don't want to spend more than five bucks. Get a feel for the very basic tricks and stunts.

Want to go further? The FireBall™can take you far, but when the string tricks call to you, you'll need another yo-yo.

Get a butterfly-shaped one, like the Cherry Bomb™. This will help you master the Mounts.

From there you need to experiment. If you're lucky, you'll have a store nearby that lets you try the yo-yos they have in stock. Or your friends may have several different types. Try them all and find your preference.

Gear

There is more stuff involved with yoing than yo-yos. Most of it is cool, but none of it is necessary. Here's a quick rundown of the things you can buy but really don't need to.

Yo-Yo Bag

You can get bags with foam core specially cut to fit your yo-yos. This is great if you're constantly trying to drag around a dozen yo-yos (trust us, it happens). If you have only two or three, then you probably only need your pockets.

When you're competing, though, it's nice to have a neat bag for toting your tools.

Holster

These clip onto your belt and keep your yo-yo always by your side. A holster fits only one yo-yo at a time.

Again, a pocket will serve you well, but a holster can look sharp when you're with your yo-yo buddies.

Finger Tape

Does the string hurt your finger? Wrap a bit of finger tape around it and you can avoid the worst of the dreaded purple finger. The tape helps stop the string from cutting off circulation to your finger.

Finger Protectors and Gloves

Finger protectors are like reusable tape. They keep your fingers from swelling up. A glove goes on your free hand and helps keep the string clean. It also reduces the friction of the string against your skin.

Quick string tricks slide more easily along the glove's surface than the surface of your skin.

Onward

That's your basic lesson on what equipment you might need.

Now you've got a yo-yo and you don't know how to feed it."Feed it?" you ask. Yes, a yo-yo needs certain care and maintenance to work properly. Check out the next section and see what we mean.

Care and Feeding

Now What?

All right, you have a yo-yo that fits your level and style. Now what?

Well, before you start yo-yoing you'll need to learn a few things about caring for your new, round pal. A neglected yo-yo can lead to lousy yo-yoing. Take a moment to give the yo-yo a once-over and make sure everything is shipshape.

Simple, But Not So Simple

On the whole, a yo-yo has a simple design. There's the heavy round bit at the bottom with a string tied to it.

Let's break it down a little more. The heavy bit, technically known as the "yo-yo body," has several parts to it: the halves, the axle, and (in some cases) the lids on the halves. Some yo-yos have springs and levers packed into the halves, but we'll stick with the basics.

Then there's the string. You might think there isn't much to a piece of string. That's true in most cases, but this is yo-yo string. You'll need to pay attention to the knot for the loop, the twist in the string, and the way the string loops around the axle.

Simple, right?

Read on and you'll learn the best techniques for caring for your yo-yo. Don't shrug off the tips below; a healthy yo-yo will spin longer, faster, and straighter and will even Loop better.

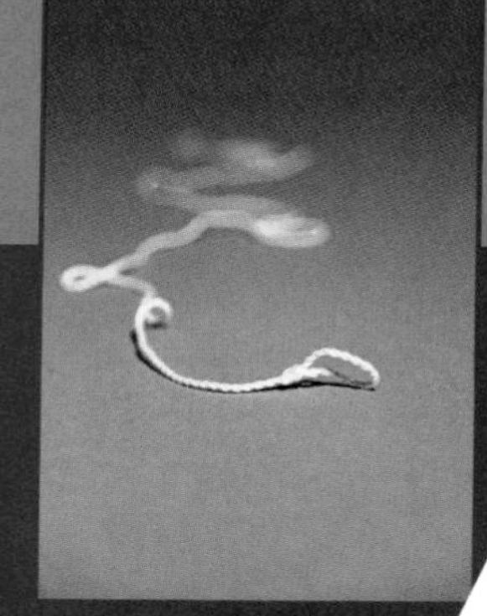

By itself, not so impressive. With a yo-yo attached, it can help you achieve greatness.

String

The string is the simplest part of the yo-yo but needs the most constant care. Many common problems can be traced to this seemingly innocuous piece of cotton.

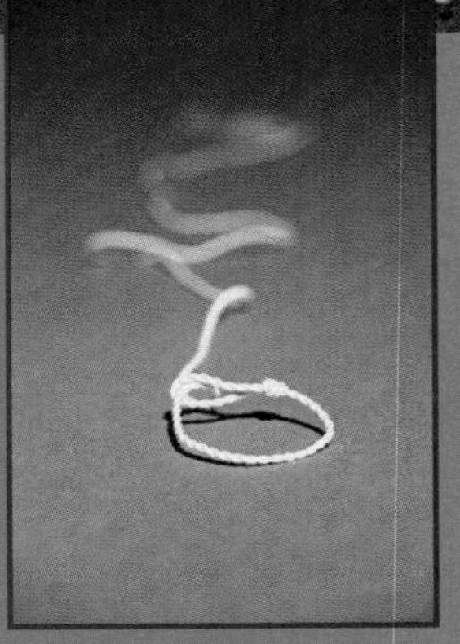

The Finger Loop

Most yo-yos come out of the package with a loop tied into the end of the string. This is *not* where you put your finger!

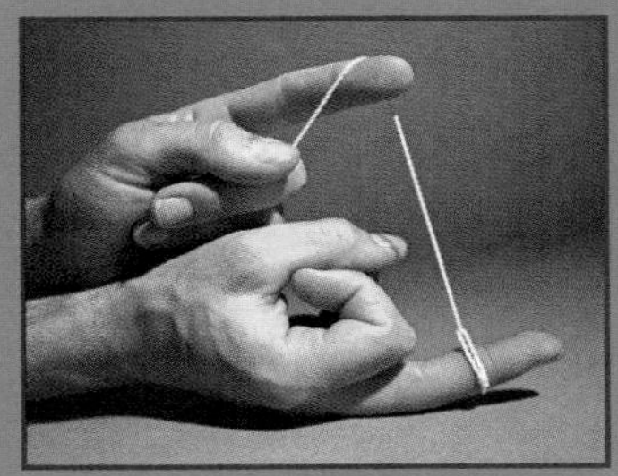

That loop is just half of the slipknot you need to make the string fit comfortably on your hand. Make the slipknot by pushing the string through the loop.

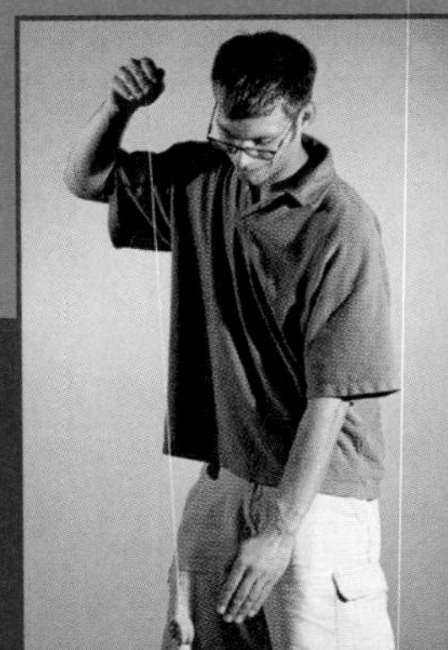

Let the yo-yo spin until it stops. This should take care of the twist problems.

Twist

Is your string binding up? Can't get it to sleep? Maybe your string is twisted too tightly. What to do? Follow these simple instructions.

- Drop the yo-yo.
- Spin the yo-yo.
- Let the yo-yo string loosen or tighten.

For a cool and fast way to loosen or tighten the string, read about the UFO trick. It will amaze your friends and will keep your string tuned up.

Knots

Kids, don't run with sharp objects. And get your parents to help you out.

Sometimes a trick goes horribly, horribly wrong and you end up with a knot in the middle of your string. This kind of knot can be extremely tight, impervious to your attempts to untie it with your fingers.

Try using a pin or needle to work the knot out. Be very careful not to stab yourself.

Sometimes your string can tie itself tightly around the axle. Don't despair! If you have a yo-yo that can unscrew, you should have no trouble fixing the problem. If the yo-yo doesn't come apart, try the needle trick to remove that pesky knot.

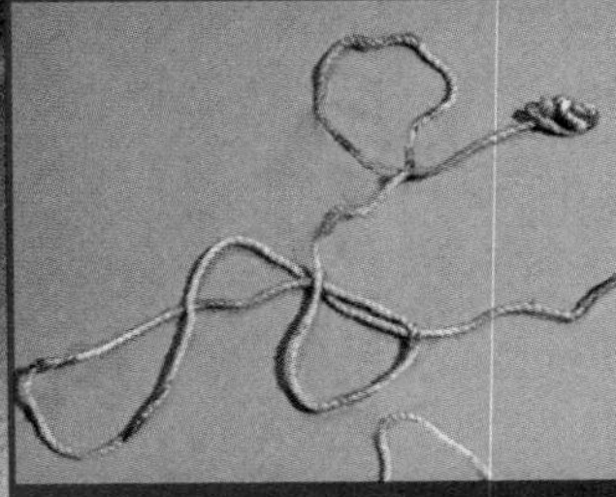

The most common problem is a dirty string. A soiled string will greatly reduce the performance of the yo-yo—especially during Loops!

Axle knots won't bother you much when you can pull your yo-yo to pieces.

TIP The correct way to get the proper string length is to let the yo-yo dangle all the way to the ground. Tie a loop where the string meets your belly-button. Cut off any extra string, and presto—it's the correct length! No more throwing the yo-yo directly into the ground.

Trivi-Yo It's believed that what we know as the yo-yo originated in China.

Breaks

More often than not, the string breaks right *next* to your finger, where it's been rubbing against the knot of your loop. It also breaks at the end of a really strong throw. If this happens, you'll watch helplessly as the yo-yo goes flying off into the sky, through a window, bounces down the street, and gets run over by a car.

Changing the string frequently can help you avoid this tragedy. Check the loop around the axle and your finger for signs of fraying and decide whether you should replace the string.

Once you've decided to change the cord, how do you do it? Follow the instructions and you'll manage it.

1. First, untwist the bottom of the string to form a loop.

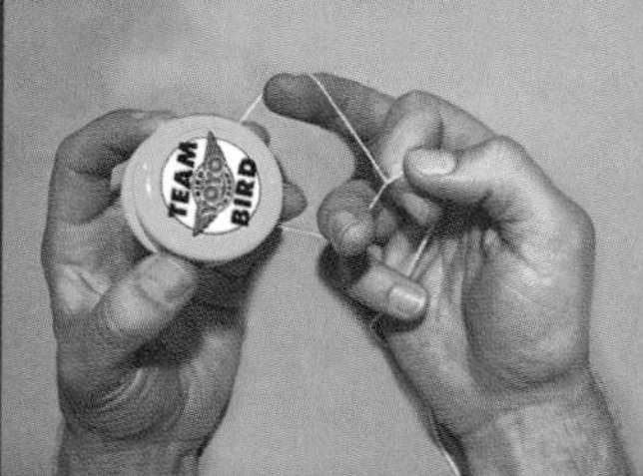

2. Next, place the loop around the yo-yo so it rests on the axle.

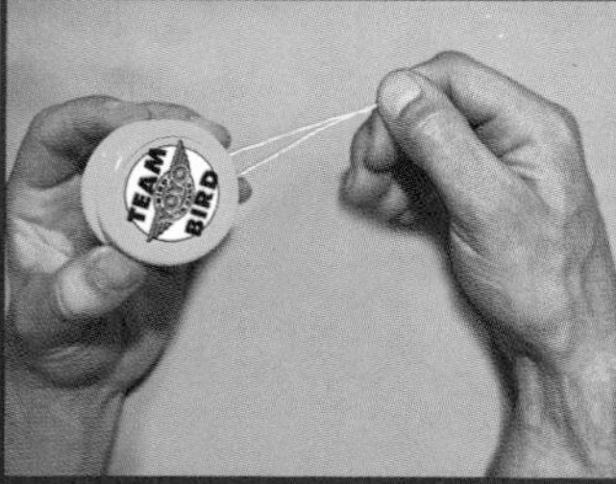

3. Finally, let the string twist back and tighten around the axle.

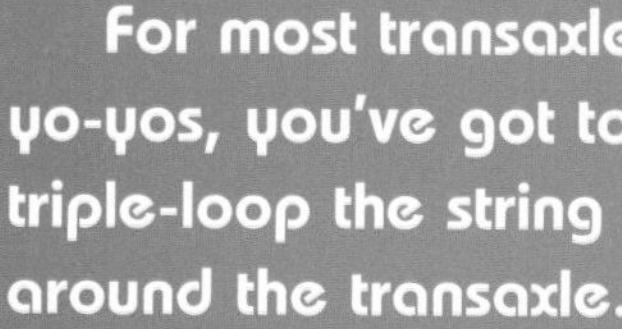

For most transaxle yo-yos, you've got to triple-loop the string around the transaxle.

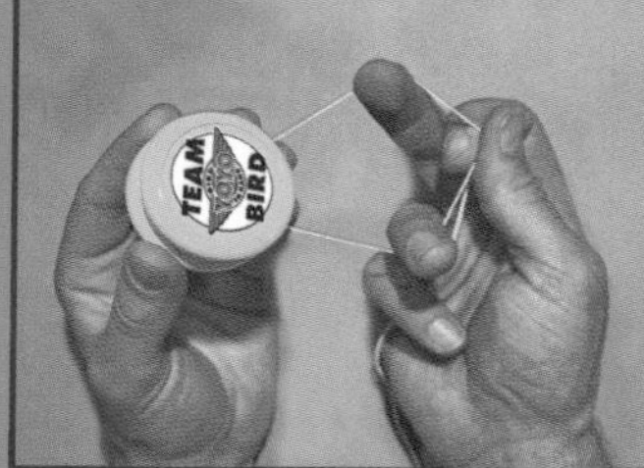

1. Start with a loop—usually known as the first loop.

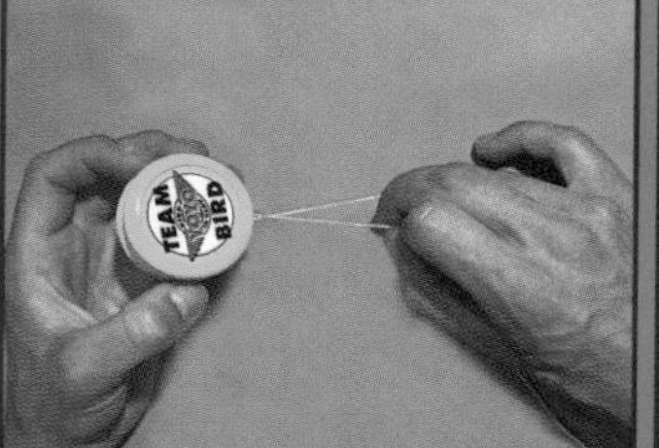

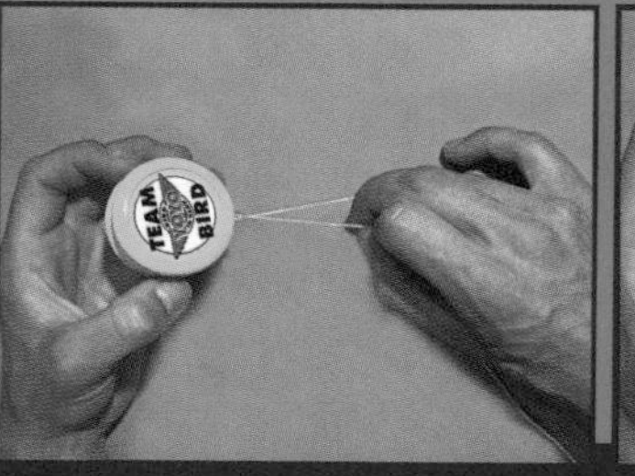

2. Twist the string and then wrap it around the yo-yo for the second loop.

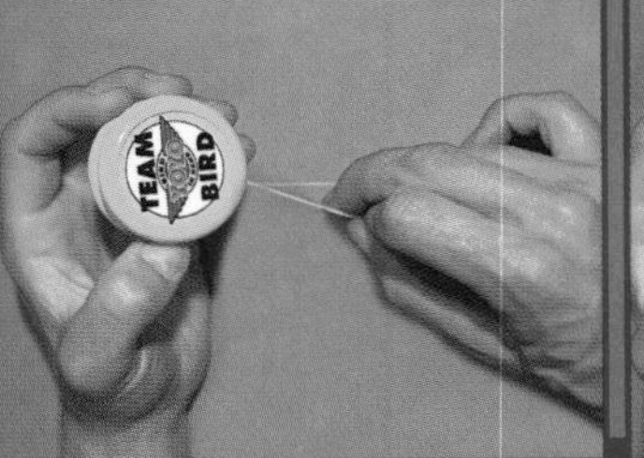

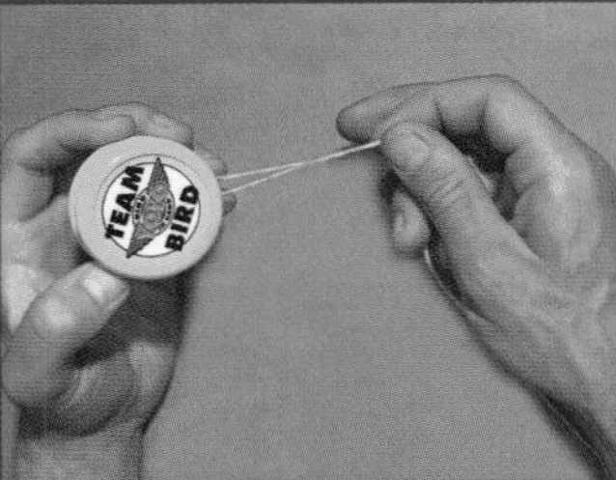

3. Twist and wrap again to get that third loop. Voila! A triple loop around your transaxle.

Check the yo-yo's instruction manual to see whether it recommends the triple loop for your yo-yo.

Trivi-Yo

Throughout history, yo-yo's have been made from many different materials. Some of these include: wood, plastic, rock, bakelite, metal, clay, and even glass!

Winding

Your yo-yo has died. For some reason, it went down and didn't come back up. How do you get the string wound up onto the axle? There are several methods to try.

The cool and snazzy way is a snap. Place the thumb and middle finger of your free hand along the string gutter. Pull the string taut and then roll your thumb off the yo-yo. It should wind at least partway up the string, allowing you to work it back up to your yo-yo hand with a few short pulls. This works best with fixed-axle yo-yos but can be pulled off with others.

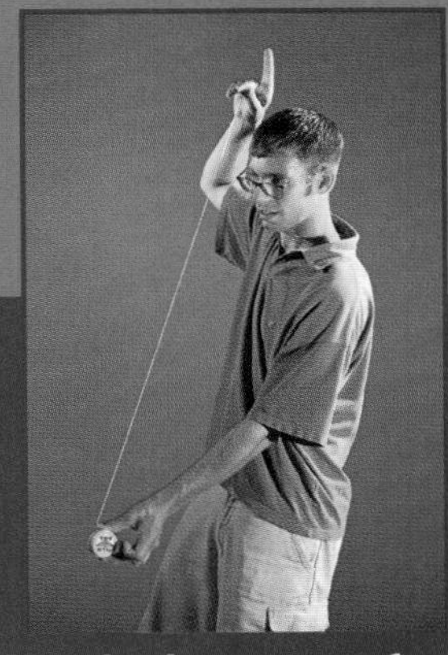

Here's the setup for a snap of a dead yo-yo.

If the snap just won't do it, you may have to manually wind the string around the axle. First, make sure you remove the loop from your finger. This ensures that you won't twist up your string while winding.

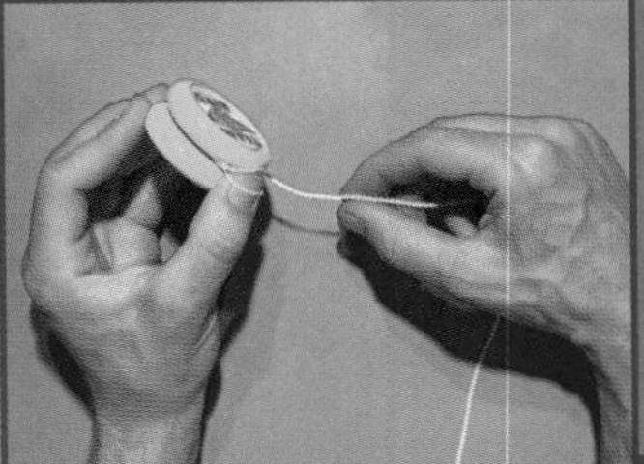

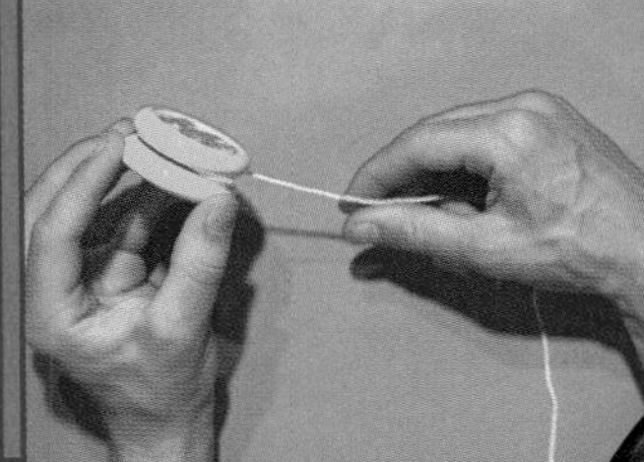

This trick works perfectly for transaxle yo-yos.

Place the index finger of your free hand over the string gutter. On the first wind, wrap the string loosely over your finger. Then wind the rest onto the axle.

This technique will let you wind up any transaxle yo-yo without trouble. Without the first pass over the finger, the string would just spin around without winding up.

On the right, you can see the fixed axle, solidly placed in the yo-yo and (usually) not meant to be unscrewed. On the left is the transaxle. The ring around it spins freely on the lubricated metal axle, allowing for longer spins.

Axles

There are lots of different types of axles. The two most common are the fixed axle and the transaxle.

The fixed axle requires little care beyond your refraining from sitting on your yo-yo. The transaxle will need lubrication. You can buy axle lube at most shops that carry yo-yos. The only trick is that you do *not* want to overdo it. Just a drop or two will be enough.

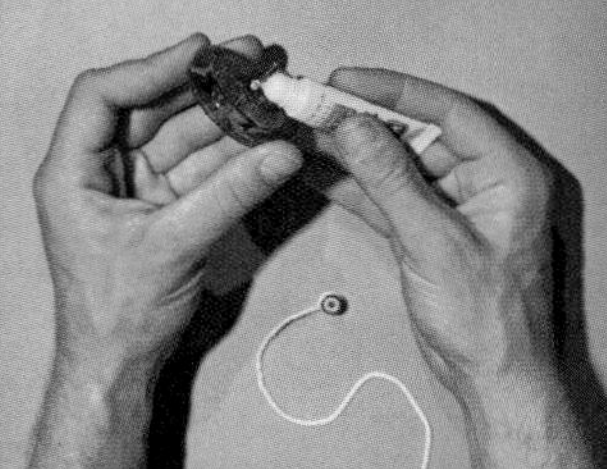

For looping tricks, try squirting petroleum jelly or name-brand axle lube onto the axle. Lip balm works great. Don't get any oil on the threads of the axle, though, or the yo-yo halves may fly apart in the middle of a trick.

Onward

All right, you now know the basics of caring for your yo-yo. Other tricks will become apparent as you get better and experiment on your own.

But enough talk! You didn't come here to hear us yap—you came here to yo! Turn the page and we'll have you throwing in no time.

Building Blocks

Gravity Pull

This is the most basic of all yo-yo moves. It's not so much a trick as the foundation on which all your yo-yoing will be built. The Gravity Pull is a quick up/down throw that most people learn soon after they buy their first yo-yos. You probably already know how to do the Gravity Pull, but are you doing it right?

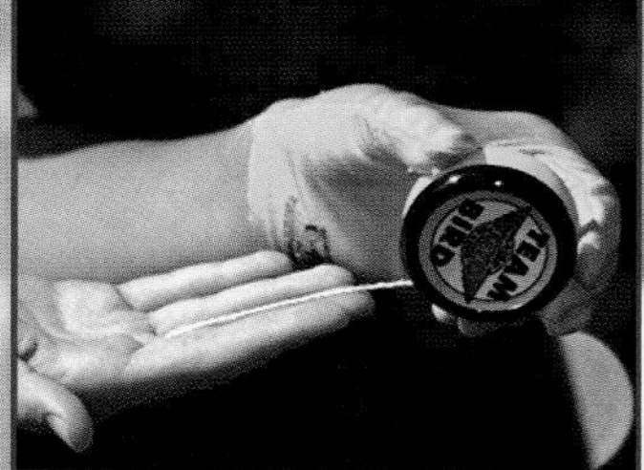

1. You MUST have the string lie this way, toward the front of your finger.

2. Now bend your arm as though you were flexing your muscles. Like Popeye, or your favorite wrestler.

3. Throw the yo-yo straight down, letting it roll off your finger and keeping your palm up. Don't turn your hand over until the yo-yo has left your fingers. You want your Gravity Pull to be straight.

4. Don't let the yo-yo sleep at the bottom of the string (see Sleeper, the next Building Block described). Turn your hand palm down and give a slight tug at the bottom of the throw to make it travel back to your hand.

5. SLAP! A strong Gravity Pull will smack into your palm with a satisfying sound. Well done!

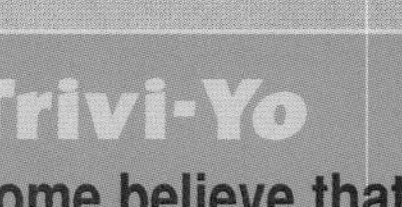

Trivi-Yo

Some believe that hunters in the Philippines used rock yo-yo's to throw at wild animals from trees. If they missed, the rock would come back. The story, sadly, isn't true.

Sleeper

The Sleeper is one of the most useful Building Blocks you can learn. Mastering the art of throwing a good, strong Sleeper will take you far toward mastering the yo-yo. Spend time working on this technique before racing ahead to other tricks, and they'll be easier when you get to them.

1. Look familiar? Start the throw as though you were doing a basic Gravity Pull. The faster you throw, the longer the yo-yo will sleep. But when you're just starting out, don't worry about throwing it REALLY hard. Concentrate on throwing it correctly. Notice the bent wrist.

2. Aim your throw about three feet in front of you, so that the yo-yo goes out at an angle. Use your wrist to flick the yo-yo. This will help build the speed of rotation, essential to a good Sleeper.

Tip: Remember, don't turn your hand over until after the yo-yo has left your fingers. If you turn your palm down too soon, the yo-yo will spin sideways. No good. Keep your palm up so the yo-yo spins straight and tricks will be easier, cleaner, and more impressive.

3. Hold your arm out when the yo-yo hits the end of the string. Do *not* tug on the string. Let the yo-yo swing back toward you a bit, then quickly pull your arm in. This should stop the yo-yo from swinging back and forth and keep it directly under your hand.

4. When you want to return the yo-yo to your hand, give the string a crisp tug and the yo-yo should snap back up. If it won't, you may need to lube the axle (on a transaxle), or tighten your string (on a fixed axle).

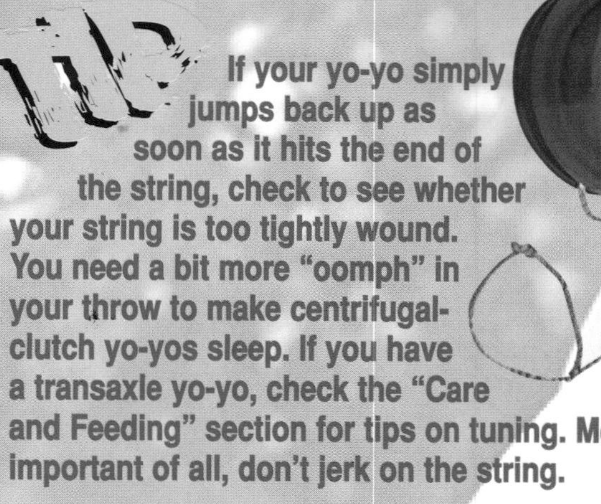

TIP If your yo-yo simply jumps back up as soon as it hits the end of the string, check to see whether your string is too tightly wound. You need a bit more "oomph" in your throw to make centrifugal-clutch yo-yos sleep. If you have a transaxle yo-yo, check the "Care and Feeding" section for tips on tuning. Most important of all, don't jerk on the string.

Forward Pass

This Building Block is also used to start many of the tricks you'll learn later on. It's also a trick all on its own and can impress folks who don't know how to yo. If you ever wanted to play catch by yourself, the gravity-defying Forward Pass is the trick for you.

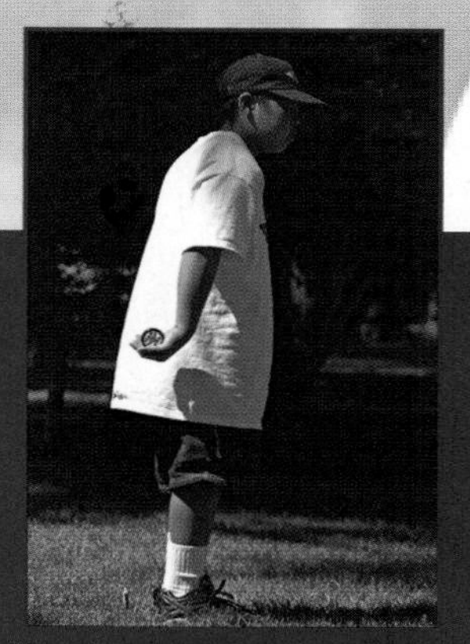

1. Start with this awkward hand position. Keep your knuckles toward the ground and cradle the yo-yo in your palm. Make sure no one is standing right in front of you!

2. Throw straight out from your body, extending your arm as shown. Let the yo-yo roll out but do not turn your hand. Hold your palm down through the first part of the throw.

3. Turn your hand palm up as the yo-yo makes its way back to you. Don't yank the string. This won't make the yo-yo come back any faster and it may just get you a bonk on the noggin. A strong throw out will make the return snappy and sharp, but don't overdo it.

4. SLAP! Again, a well-thrown Forward Pass will make a solid sound when it returns to your hand.

TIP Once again, remember that the string should roll off your fingers as it did in the Gravity Pull. Unless we tell you otherwise, always assume that the string position is the same.

Inside Loop

The Inside Loop actually begins with a Forward Pass, but because it's such a big part of many other tricks, we put it under the Building Block category. The Loop will probably be your first big challenge. You'll need a steady arm, a supple wrist, and a well-tuned yo-yo to get it right.

There are Outside Loops, but we'll get to those later. Inside Loops are more important for building tricks.

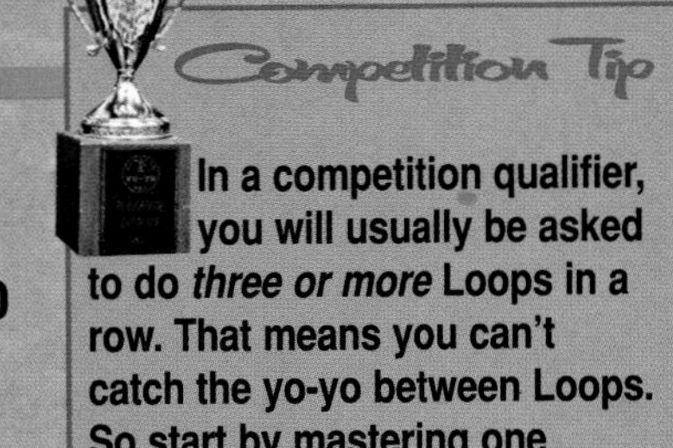

Competition Tip

In a competition qualifier, you will usually be asked to do *three or more* Loops in a row. That means you can't catch the yo-yo between Loops. So start by mastering one Loop, then work your way up. With practice, you can Loop until the cows come home.

1. Set up and start just as you would for a Forward Pass. However ...

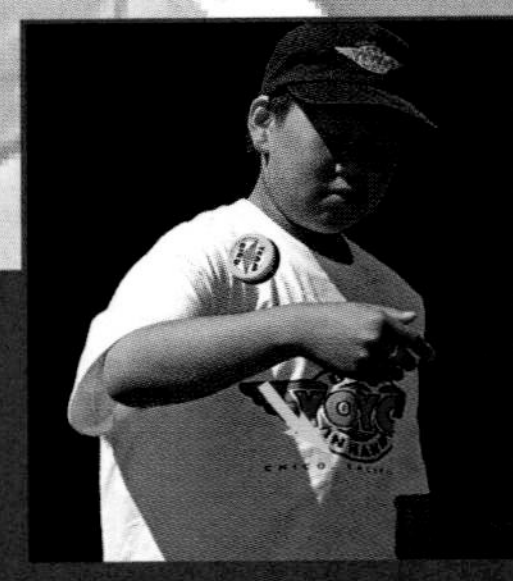

2. Don't catch the yo-yo when it comes back to your hand. Instead, let your wrist guide it over your hand and around. Keep the yo-yo on the inside of your arm.

TIP For a proper, basic Inside Loop, the yo-yo *must* travel around on the inside, between your body and your arm. It's a little spooky, but it's the correct way to throw an Inside Loop. If you're scared, wear a motorcycle helmet or catcher's mask while practicing.

3. A flick of the wrist sends the yo-yo back out into a Forward Pass. The Loop is all in the wrist. You need to make a motion like you're unscrewing a lightbulb. Do not move your arm back and forth, keep all the motion in your hand and wrist.

4. Catch the yo-yo as it comes back and—BINGO!—you've completed one loop.

Competition Tip

Some competitions require "Loop-Offs" as tie-breakers. In Loop-Offs, the contestants must do as many *perfect* Inside Loops as possible. No loss of control, no corkscrewing string, and no Outside Loops are allowed. See the sections on intermediate-level tricks for more tips on continuous Looping.

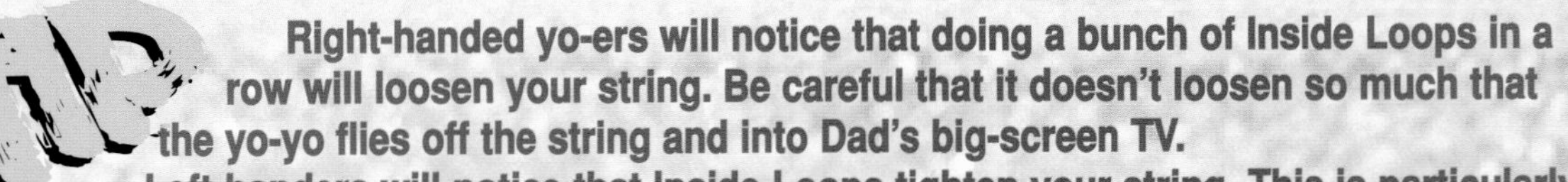

TIP Right-handed yo-ers will notice that doing a bunch of Inside Loops in a row will loosen your string. Be careful that it doesn't loosen so much that the yo-yo flies off the string and into Dad's big-screen TV.

Left-handers will notice that Inside Loops tighten your string. This is particularly important if you're using a fixed-axle yo-yo. If the string tightens too much, the yo-yo will stop spinning altogether.

Break Away

Remember the Sleeper? The Break Away uses the same type of action except that it's out to the side rather than in front of you. This move will also show up time and time again in later tricks. As with all the Building Blocks, practice, practice, practice.

1. As with the Gravity Pull and the Sleeper, start your windup by flexing a muscle. This time, however, flex it to the side.

2. Throw the yo-yo off to the side and then relax your hand so that the yo-yo sleeps before it swings across your body. Notice that your arm should not straighten out. Keep a slight bend in your elbow.

Trivi-Yo The record for the longest sleeper is always getting longer. Can you get a yo-yo to sleep for more than three minutes?

TIP Don't worry about the yo-yo making it across your body. Concentrate on throwing it out to the side, and it will swing all by itself.

3. Let the yo-yo swing across your body. Your arm should track the yo-yo as it swings, but you shouldn't pull it. Remember to let it swing by itself.

4. Right about here is where you want the Break Away to end. Give the string a tug and the yo-yo will reel back toward your hand.

5. Right back to you. That's the Break Away.

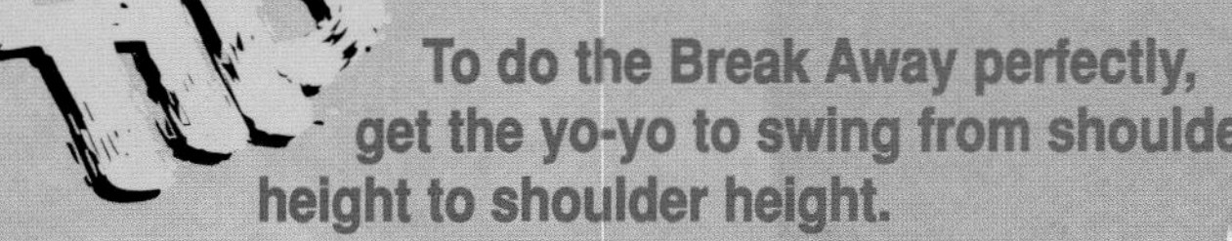

TIP To do the Break Away perfectly, get the yo-yo to swing from shoulder height to shoulder height.

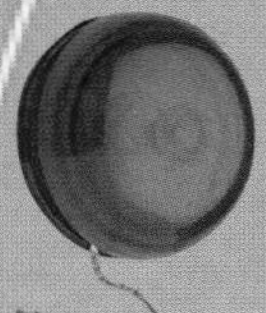

Moving On

Now, have you mastered the Building Blocks? All of them? Some of them?

Are you ready for the beginning tricks? If so, read on. If you're still shaky on some of the Building Blocks ... don't despair—read on!

Remember, though, that if a trick is giving you trouble, it's always good to check the icons next to the name. If you just can't get the 3 Leaf Clover to work, for example, look at the Building Block icons next to it: Loop and Gravity Pull. Maybe the problem is in your Loop. Then come back to this section and practice your Loop.

Once you're back on track with the Building Blocks, go back to that hard trick and see whether it's easier.

Yo-yoing is all about three words: practice, practice, practice.

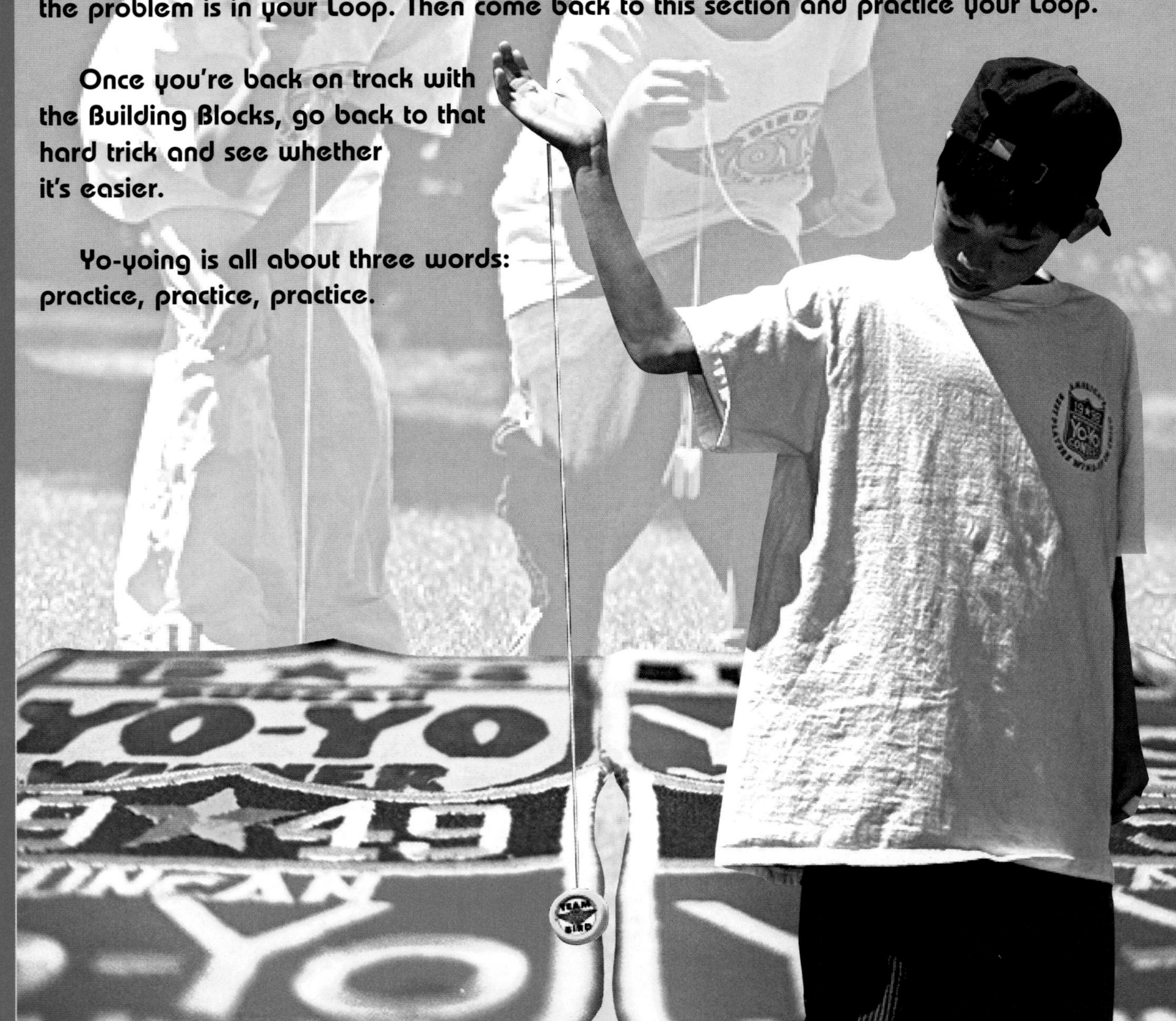

Tricks

Here you'll find a large helping of tricks that you can do with almost any yo-yo. These tricks may seem easy to some yo-ers, but remember that even the Yo-Yo Masters started with simple maneuvers. Even the most basic tricks can show up in the highest levels of competition. So, study hard and learn them all.

Walk the Dog

A very old and respectable trick. Who hasn't heard of Walk the Dog? Abbie Hoffman once Walked the Dog all the way across a congressional chamber during a hearing. (Ask your parents who Abbie Hoffman was.) As you can see by the icon, you'll need to know the Sleeper to pull this trick off.

1. Start with a hard and fast Sleeper. Be careful not to simply hurl the yo-yo straight into the ground, or you'll end up with a broken yo-yo.

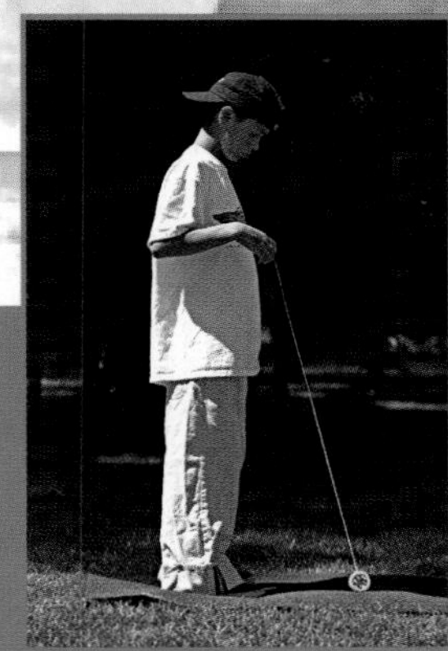

2. Gently set the yo-yo down. Don't let the string go loose; you want the yo-yo to just barely touch the ground.

3. If you want to take a longer walk, simply move to keep up with your "dog." Don't let it run too long or it won't come back.

4. When you're done, give a quick tug and the pooch will "heel"—all the way home.

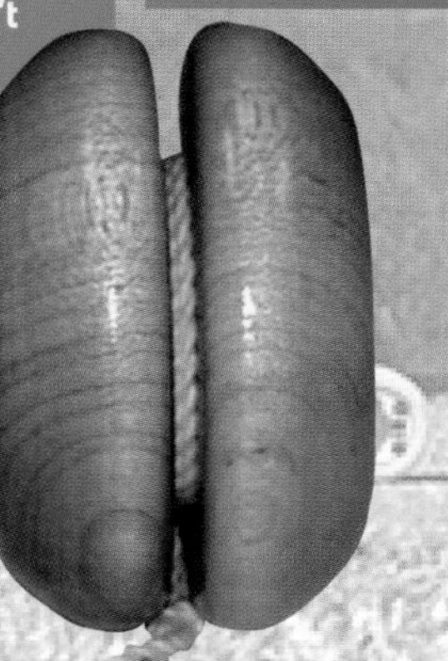

TIP You can do this trick on a piece of paper to create a buzz saw sound. Or, if you don't mind getting wet, do it over a puddle and watch the water fly!

Walk the Cat

We all know that dogs love to be walked. Put 'em on a leash and they're happy. A cat, however, is not much fun on a leash. This trick shows the difference between the two animals.

1. As with Walk the Dog, start with a fast Sleeper.

2. Walk around the yo-yo, letting it stay in the exact same place. Don't lower it to the ground until you've moved to the other side.

3. Touch the yo-yo down and watch it shoot behind you. Now either walk forward and take the "cat" for a drag or walk backward as if being pulled back by your surly pet.

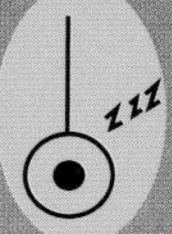

Dragster

This is another fun trick that probably won't show up in any serious competition. The Dragster, also known as "Running the Dog," is great for racing with your friends or playing with your cat.

TIP

You can get a group of friends together and have Dragster races.

1. Throw a fast Sleeper (sound familiar?), but don't touch the yo-yo to the ground yet. With your free hand, undo the loop around your finger. You may want to loosen the loop before you throw the Sleeper.

2. Now touch the yo-yo to the ground (don't drop it, just lower it gently) and let go of the string. The yo-yo will speed away!

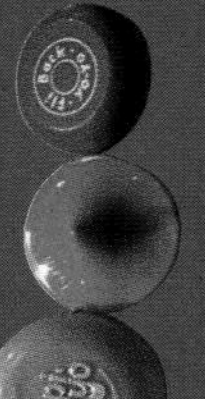

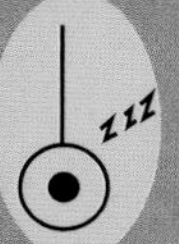

Creeper (Basic and Advanced)

The Creeper is a competition trick. It's challenging enough to have tripped up some very skilled yo-ers during their qualifiers. Don't worry if you don't get it on the first try.

1. Begin with a Sleeper and then swing the yo-yo out in front of you. Keep your hand low because ...

2. ... you need to then lower the yo-yo onto the ground and let it sleep there for a second. Bring the string all the way down as well.

3. Place your hand, palm up, on the ground. Give the string a little jerk and the yo-yo will creep back along the ground and into your hand. That's the Basic Creeper.

4. An Advanced Creeper is when the yo-yo is on the ground the *whole* time. Rather than swinging the yo-yo out and then letting it roll back, you must walk the yo-yo out along the ground first. Except for that, it's just like the Basic.

TIP Remember to keep your hand on the ground to catch the yo-yo on its way back. Don't count on it just hopping up the string. If you miss it in a competition, you'll get marked down points for loss of control (see the chapter on competitions).

Trivi-Yo

The yo-yo's popularity goes up and down—much like a yo-yo. Unlike other fads—pet rocks, hula hoops, pogs—yo-yos *keep* coming back!

Competition Tip

In competition, you can't get away with just the Basic Creeper. If you're asked to do a Creeper, the judges mean the Advanced Creeper.

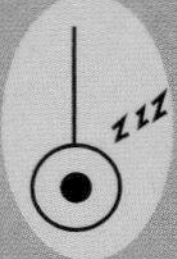

Around the World

Look out and make room! Around the World is a big trick that needs a lot of space. It's an easy trick to perform but is very impressive to watch.

1. Start this off with a Forward Pass. Throw the yo-yo extra hard to start it sleeping at the end of the string.

2. Let the momentum of your yo-yo carry it around your hand. Hardly any movement of your hand is needed to keep the yo-yo orbiting. You shouldn't have to move your arm at all.

3. When the yo-yo has completed a full orbit, give the string a tug and the yo-yo will return from its travels.

TIP You can do more than one orbit before tugging the string. Try to see how many you can do and still get the yo-yo to return. Be careful! The string can break easily when you give the yo-yo a hard toss! Try it with a new string.

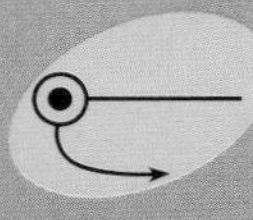
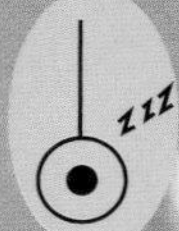

World Tour

The World Tour is almost identical to Around the World. The only difference is that instead of orbiting the yo-yo to your side, you orbit it in front of you.

1. Start with a regular Break Away, but instead of just going from shoulder height to shoulder height, keep going! Let the yo-yo orbit around in a full circle.

TIP The World Tour is actually safer than Around the World because your yo-yo doesn't go behind you. You can therefore see where your yo-yo is going and you won't smack someone by accident.

2. When you've done an orbit and a half (or more if you want), tug the string and let the yo-yo return from its World Tour.

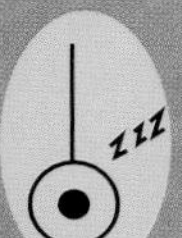

Rock the Baby

Another classic and often-requested trick. This is one that you can, and probably should, practice while the yo-yo is "dead." That is to say, while it's not spinning. So, unravel the yo-yo and go through the motions.

1. Throw a strong Sleeper (when you're doing it for real). Hold the string close to your body and bring your free hand to about the middle of the string.

2. Fold the string over your free hand, right at the base of your fingers. Then pinch the string with your yo-yo hand, usually about five inches from the yo-yo itself.

3. Now push your free hand forward and down while bringing your yo-yo hand slightly up. Your free hand should rest palm up, as though you were holding a plate. Once you're in position, rock that baby!

TIP You can get *out* of Rock the Baby by simply doing the motions backward. Or, if the Baby is spinning fast enough, you can lightly toss the yo-yo away from you. Let go of the string as you toss and it should rewind into your hand in a flash.

Rocket

Rocket is a dynamic trick but is very simple to do. For safety's sake, don't practice this trick inside (you might break something important) and don't do it over concrete (you might break your yo-yo).

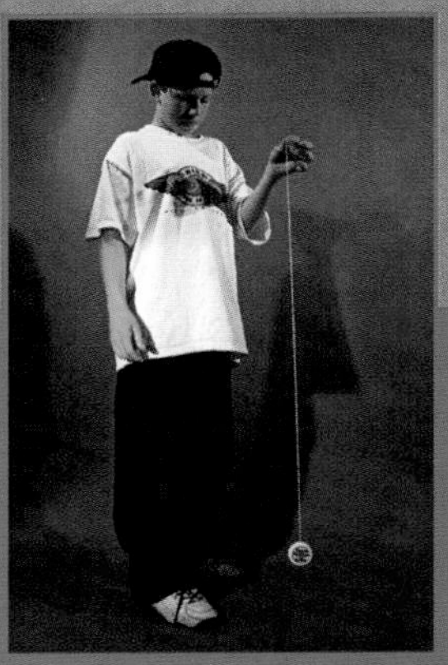

1. Guess what? Throw a fast Sleeper! Then, as for the Dragster, remove the loop from your finger.

2. Give a quick, sharp tug on the string to get the yo-yo traveling back to your hand. But don't catch it! Give an extra little flick and let go of the string at the last second. Watch the yo-yo rocket into the stratosphere … then catch it before it crashes!

TIP-For extra style and an exciting end to a performance, practice doing a Rocket in the Pocket. Do a Rocket as normal, but catch it in a large shirt or pants pocket when it comes back down. Tricky, but worth it if you can pull it off!

Tidal Wave (Skin the Cat)

Tidal Wave is a snappy little trick that we will build on in the intermediate-level chapters. The first part is slow and the second part is quick. The combination is a good one and worth learning.

1. Once the yo-yo is sleeping peacefully at the end of the string, bring the index finger of your free hand against the string finger on your yo-yo hand. Make sure the fingers are parallel.

2. At the same time, reach your free hand's index finger out and slightly up while your string finger pulls back and slightly down. Don't be in a rush. Let the string come back slowly. You should get this angle in the string.

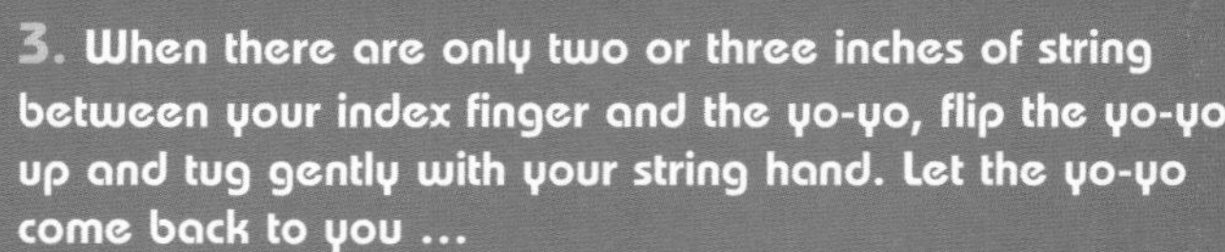

3. When there are only two or three inches of string between your index finger and the yo-yo, flip the yo-yo up and tug gently with your string hand. Let the yo-yo come back to you …

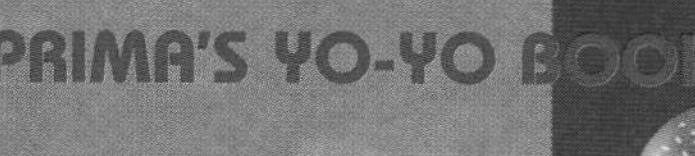

4. But don't catch it! Let it swing under your hand and then flick it out again into a Loop. Once it has made the full Loop, let the yo-yo come back to rest in your waiting palm. Ta-daaa!

Trivi-Yo

The word yo-yo comes from the Filipino language called Tagalog. It means, "come, come" or "come back," which is exactly what a yo-yo does.

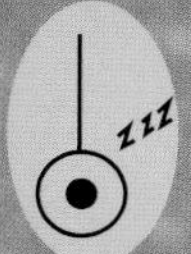

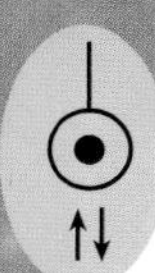

Around the Corner (Pop the Clutch)

Another trick with two names. This one bends your arm in weird ways. Follow the pictures and you should be all right.

1. As with so many of these tricks, start with a fast Sleeper. Then turn your hand palm up and bring the string to the outside of your arm.

2. Now bring your hand back so the string is almost behind your back, about midway between your elbow and your shoulder. Once it's there, bring your hand down so the string drapes over your upper arm, as in the picture.

3. Pinch the string a little bit above the yo-yo. Give it a small tug—and *let go*!

4. The yo-yo will pop up over your shoulder and fall back down. Don't catch it; let it fall past your hand ...

5. Then guide it into a Gravity Pull to get it back to your hand. You've successfully popped the clutch.

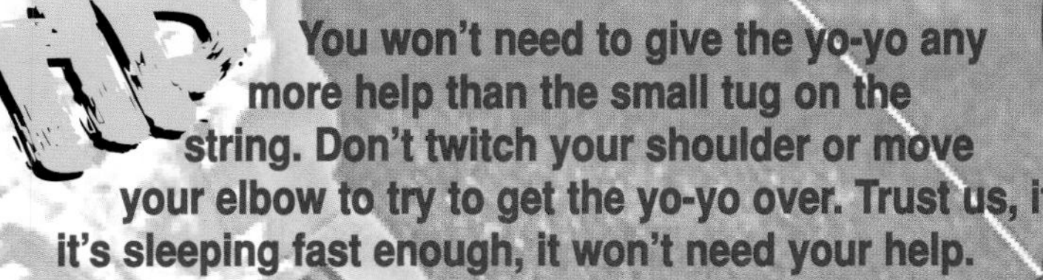

You won't need to give the yo-yo any more help than the small tug on the string. Don't twitch your shoulder or move your elbow to try to get the yo-yo over. Trust us, if it's sleeping fast enough, it won't need your help.

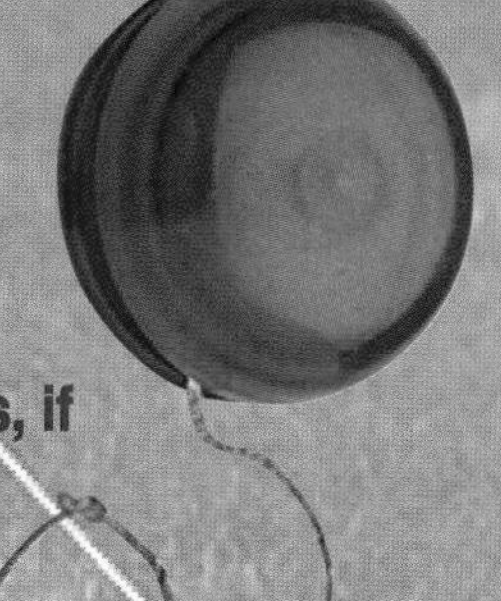

BEGINNING TRICKS

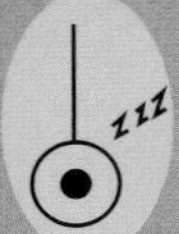

Elevator

Take note that Elevator is the first "string trick" in the book. In later chapters, most of the tricks you'll learn will be string tricks, or "String Mounts." So take special care to get the feel of the yo-yo resting against the string in this trick and Monkey on a String.

1. Start with a strong Sleeper. Take the index finger of your free hand and place it under your yo-yo finger between your body and the string. Raise your index finger so the string runs over it and the yo-yo is outside. Do this until the yo-yo is two inches above your yo-yo hand.

2. Now lean your index finger back so the yo-yo straddles the string.

3. Pull up with your free hand and down with your throw hand until the yo-yo is about two inches away from your free hand.

4. Flick your free hand up so the yo-yo pops up. This should make it catch on the string and wind back down into your hand. Voila! The Elevator.

TIP String tricks are much easier with a butterfly-type yo-yo. You can save yourself a lot of frustration by using this type of yo-yo when you're practicing string tricks.

Monkey on a String

Almost identical to Elevator. The only difference is that the yo-yo is on the other side of the string in Monkey on a String.

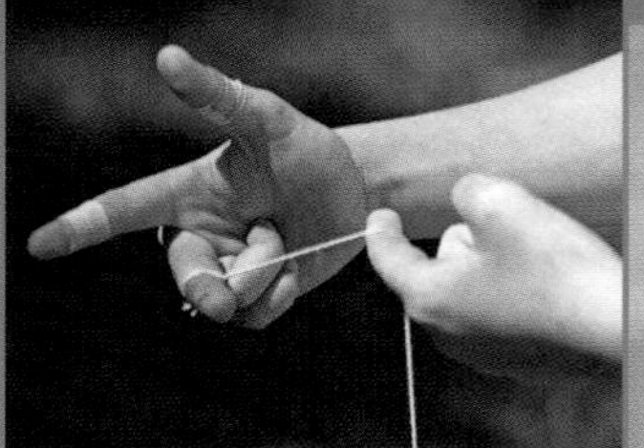

1. Do everything the same as when you're doing the Elevator except place the index finger of your free hand on the *outside* of the string. The string should be between your body and your free hand.

2. Keep the yo-yo on the inside of the string. Then follow all the same steps you followed for the Elevator. A small difference, but it makes for a whole new trick.

Over the Falls

Over the Falls has a quick change in direction that can really wow your audience. Take extra practice time to get this move clean and precise. The sharper it is, the better it will look.

1. Start Over the Falls as you would start a Loop, with a Forward Pass. This time, however, fully extend your arm.

2. As the yo-yo returns, pull your arm in.

3. When the yo-yo comes back, loop it over your hand and *straight down* your leg. This puts you right into the Gravity Pull! Congratulations, you've just gone Over the Falls.

TIP If you're pointing your hand straight down your leg but the yo-yo keeps going a little in front of you, try pointing your hand a bit behind you. This should make the yo-yo go where it's supposed to—*straight down.*

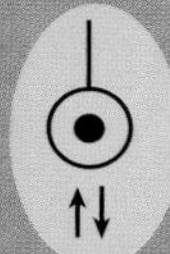

3 Leaf Clover

The 3 Leaf Clover adds onto Over the Falls. The hard part is to not just do three Loops. Again, you want this trick to be clean and sharp.

TIP You may want to practice each piece of this trick separately before putting the pieces together. You already know Over the Falls, so practice the vertical pass (straight up) first. Then practice doing the "L" loop (straight up and then into a Forward Pass). After you've mastered that, just tack on Over the Falls and you have it!

Competition Tip

Don't let all of this talk about "loops" confuse you. The 3 Leaf Clover should be more angular than circular. Remember, clean and sharp. In a competition, the last part has to come down *right next* to your foot or it does not count.

1. To start this trick, you have to defy gravity. Throw the yo-yo as straight up as you can (above a 45-degree angle is fine). The throw must be strong enough to allow the yo-yo to wind back down the string rather than just falling. Good luck!

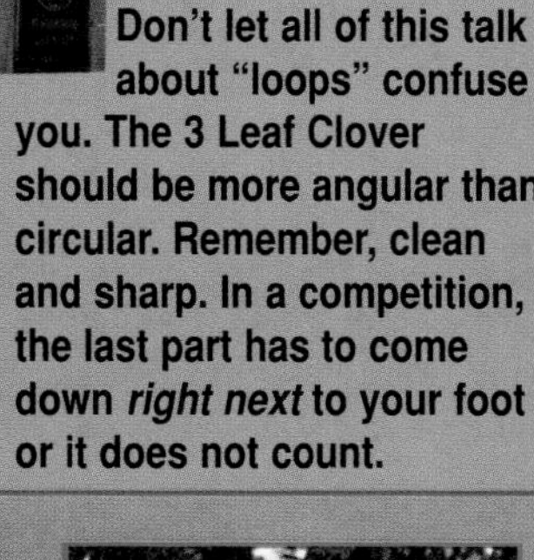

2. Let the yo-yo loop over your hand and, without catching it, send it out into a Forward Pass. Keep it straight.

3. Now it's just like Over the Falls. Let the yo-yo come back from the Forward Pass and loop over your hand, then send it straight down your leg.

Hop the Fence

This trick is like a continuous Gravity Pull. Toss the yo-yo down as you would with a Pull. When it comes back up, send it back down. Here, we'll show you ...

1. Start with a normal Gravity Pull. Throw the yo-yo down and let it come back up. However ...

2. Don't catch it! Cock your wrist back and "hop" the yo-yo over your hand. Then send it back down.

3. Continue this pattern and you'll be doing Hop the Fence.

TIP Don't let the yo-yo swing as it hops. Keep it going in a controlled looping motion.

You'll notice that the yo-yo flips over each time it hops. For righties, the string will tighten; for lefties, it will loosen. That's the opposite of Loops!

Planet Hop

Sometimes this trick is mistaken for Hop the Fence. However, you'll soon see how Planet Hop is different.

TIP Think of the Planet Hop as making the yo-yo do an upside-down "U." You don't need to be rough with your pulls. Take them slow and gentle and they should work out.

1. As with Hop the Fence, start with a Gravity Pull that you don't intend to catch.

2. This time, let it come back and loop over the *outside* of your hand so that the yo-yo is traveling (briefly) toward your body.

3. Let the yo-yo fall back down, but as it comes back toward your hand, make it loop over the *inside* of your hand. Let it travel away from your body. Repeat this pattern to do the Planet Hop.

Moving On

So now you've finished the beginners' tricks. So far, we've gone easy on you. Things only get tougher from here on out.

Once again, don't feel bad if you're not the Yo-Yo Wizard of all time yet. Given enough time and practice, you'll make it.

Meanwhile, take a peek at the intermediate tricks. Some of them may speak to you, just begging to be tried. But don't forget your roots. The beginning tricks will be here for you to review and study.

Intermediate Building Blocks

More Basics!

The Intermediate Building Blocks are a taste of what's to come. You can do most of the Intermediate tricks without knowing the Intermediate Building Blocks. However, learning the Blocks shown in this section will get you warmed up for the Advanced Building Blocks and tricks.

And, besides, the Intermediate Building Blocks are impressive all by themselves.

Building Blocks

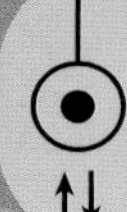

Basic Front Mount

The Basic Front Mount is a full-on string trick. In fact, any Building Block or trick with the word "Mount" in it is a string trick. In the Mounts, your yo-yo will straddle and ride the string—even multiple times!

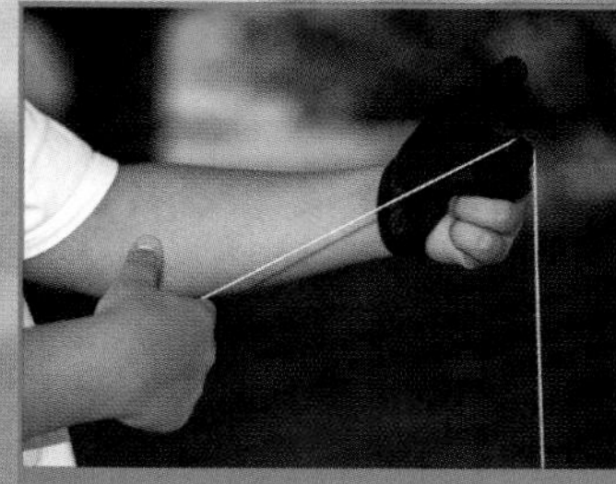

1. Start as you would for a Tidal Wave. Throw a Sleeper, put the index finger of your free hand against the string, and push it away from your body while pulling down with your yo-yo hand.

2. Pull your yo-yo a little more than halfway up the string.

3. Now move your yo-yo hand forward and catch the still-sleeping yo-yo on the string. Keep bringing your hand forward in a circular motion.

TIP Learn to master the spin. If you try to move your yo-yo hand up, the yo-yo will grind against the string. Let the yo-yo start high and drop down into the Mount. That way, the spin will be with you always.

TIP Once your free hand gets to shoulder height, it shouldn't move much. Not even during the dismount.

4. Keep bringing that yo-yo hand down so that it rests just below the free-hand index finger. If the yo-yo is *still* sleeping, you've just completed the Basic Front Mount. If it's dead, well ... try again.

TIP Keep your fingers parallel and the string lined up with the yo-yo throughout the Basic Front Mount.

Actually, you should keep those fingers parallel for just about every Mount you do. This will keep the string in line and make it easier to get the yo-yo onto it.

Imagine a vertical plane right down the middle of your body (ouch!). Your parallel fingers must remain in that plane.

Trivi-Yo

Yo-yo's were spotted in Europe in the 18th century. The French nobility was especially fond of them.

Roll Out Dismount

All right, you've done the Basic Front Mount. Now what? You could simply unwind for a Drop Dismount. Read the instructions for the Basic Front Mount in reverse and bring your hands back the way they came. But where's the pizzazz in that?

1. Let's do the Roll Out Dismount and wow the folks watching at home. Swing the yo-yo slightly (very slightly) back toward your body to get a little momentum going.

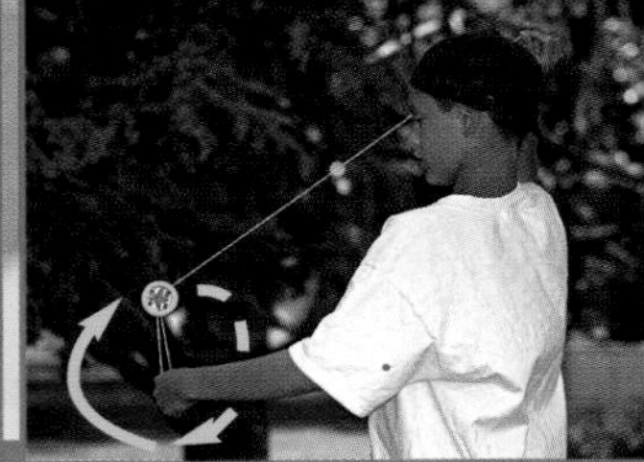

2. Swing the yo-yo out and around while you pull your yo-yo hand up and back. Remember, don't move that free hand. Keeping it still will make the trick easier. Just pull back with the yo-yo hand and everything will be peachy. Trust us.

3. As the yo-yo turns, it will unwrap from your free hand. Let it go and watch it shoot out into a Forward Pass. Give a tug with your yo-yo hand and the yo-yo will return. That's the Roll Out, a classy Dismount.

Man on the Flying Trapeze

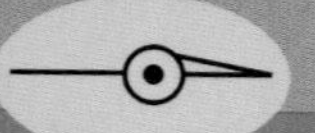

This Intermediate Building Block grows out of a Beginning Building Block, the Break Away. There's a little twist to it, however, that makes the Man on the Flying Trapeze a sweet move and a nice Mount. We'll cover a few of the Dismounts here, but this Building Block lends itself to improvisation. See what you can come up with.

1. Start with a standard Break Away. Throw to the side and let the yo-yo swing. However, stick out the index finger of your free hand. Keep it near waist level and out only as far as your yo-yo hand.

2. Let the string hit the finger of your free hand and loop over it. The yo-yo's momentum should carry it up and over—you don't need to help it along.

3. Catch the yo-yo on the string (still sleeping, of course) and you've done it! If you slide your hands closer together, the yo-yo will settle into the middle of the string.

TIP A common mistake made by yo-ers trying to learn the Man on the Flying Trapeze is to make a *big* loop and try to catch the yo-yo in the middle of the string. This will cause major frustration because it leaves so much room for error. Keep that first loop over your free hand small. Then bring your hands together to get the yo-yo to the middle.

Drop Dismount

1. Raise your free hand and lower your yo-hand so the yo-yo is no longer mounted on the string.

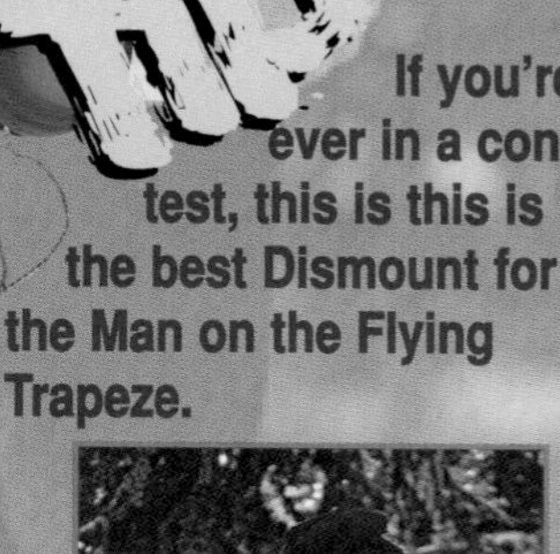

TIP If you're ever in a contest, this is this is the best Dismount for the Man on the Flying Trapeze.

2. Lower the yo-yo off of the string.

3. Catch the yo-yo for an easy Man on the Flying Trapeze Dismount.

TIP Work on getting a straight Break Away by practicing a few World Tours. Once you've mastered the World Tour, you can continue on to your Man on the Flying Trapeze training.

Back Off Dismount

Another Man on the Flying Trapeze Dismount is called the Back Off. Nothing too fancy in this one, just follow along.

1. Start with the Man on the Flying Trapeze, of course. The Back Off works best with a smaller loop; if you use too big a loop, your Dismount will look like a Fly Away (we'll get to that). Give the string a little tug and pop the yo-yo up and around.

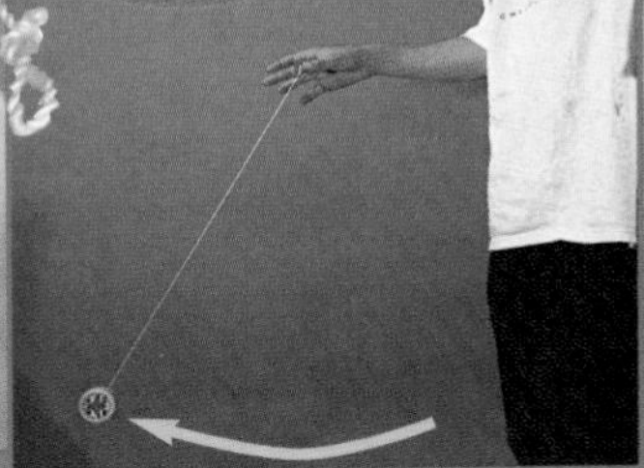

2. Let the yo-yo swing and tug it to return it to your hand. That's the Back Off.

Fly Away

A bit more dramatic than the Back Off, the Fly Away is a snappy Dismount. Do not practice this one in a room with low ceilings.

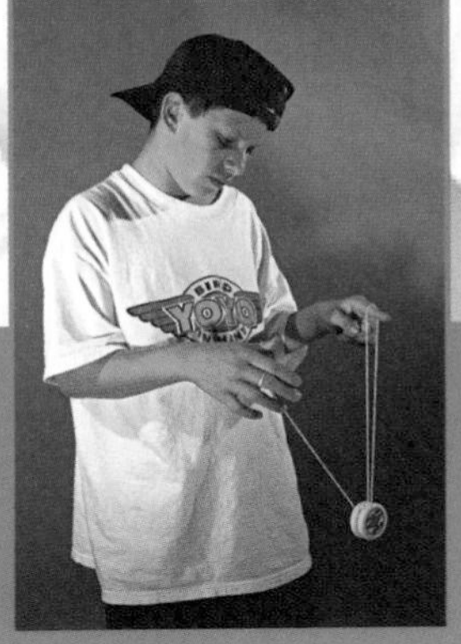

1. Do the Man on the Flying Trapeze again. This time, bring your hands closer together so the string sags and the yo-yo rests in the center.

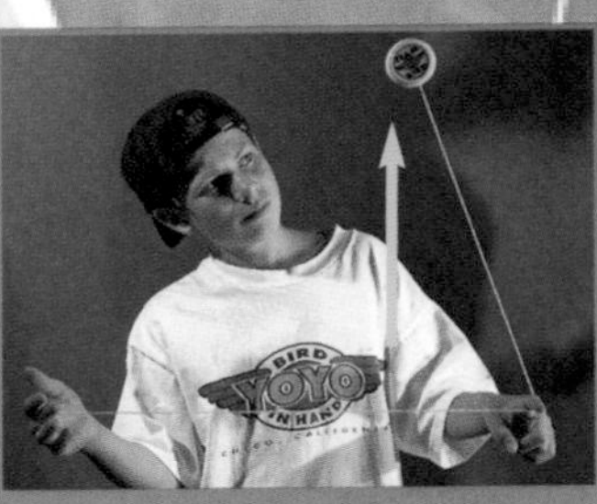

2. Now quickly pull your hands apart and launch the yo-yo into the air. *Let go* with you free hand as soon as the yo-yo leaves the string.

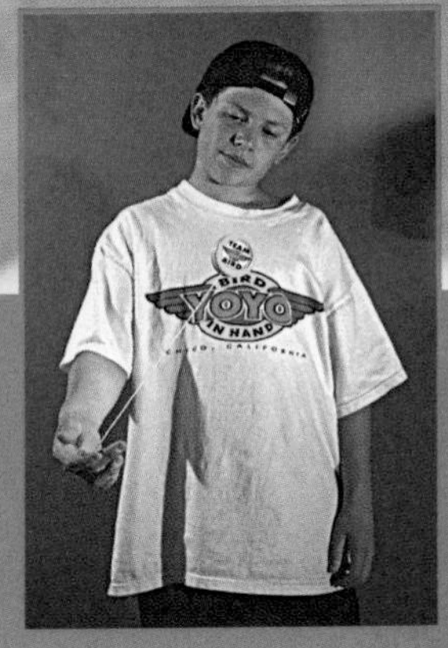

3. Watch the yo-yo Fly Away before giving it a small tug to return it to your hand.

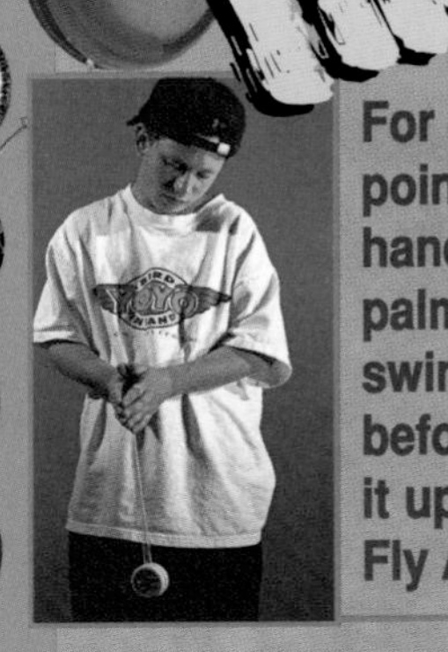

TIP

For extra style points, bring your hands together, palms flat, and swing the yo-yo before sending it up for the Fly Away.

Moving On

That ends your first course in string Mounts and Dismounts. Don't worry, there's much more to come.

The Intermediate tricks may seem simple when you first go over them. Don't be fooled. They require excellent control and, sometimes, lightning speed.

Most of all, though, they're fun! They go beyond the basic tricks that most people know. You'll hear many oohs and aahs when you pull off a Dizzy Baby and a Brain Twister.

Make no mistake, these are Intermediate tricks. Be kind to yourself and set aside lots of practice time.

Tricks

You'll see a trend in these tricks. They have a *lot* to do with string. If you're an experienced yo-er, this may come as no surprise. If you're just starting out, you might be surprised to learn how important the string is (outside of just making the yo-yo work, that is).

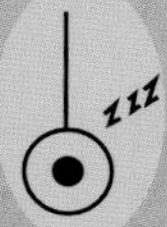

UFO

This is a maintenance trick, used to tighten or loosen your string. If you do the UFO correctly, it will look like you messed up. It is only when you return the yo-yo to your hand, that it will be clear you actually meant to do it that way.

TIP

Here you can see a string that is way too loose and one that is way too tight. Either one will have a bad effect on your tricks and general yo-yoing. Right-handers will mostly need to loosen their strings, and lefties will need to tighten.

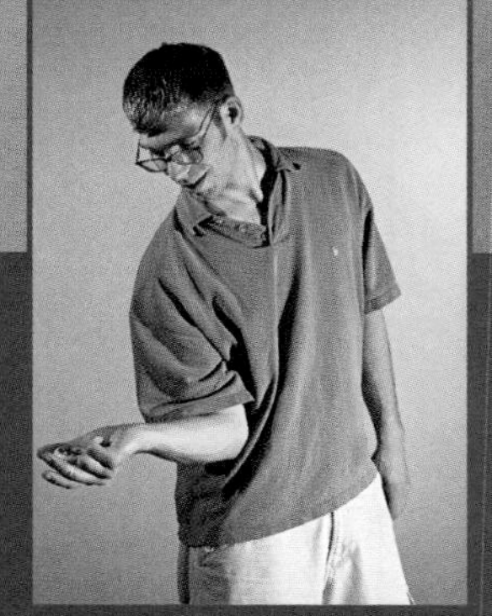

1. Start with your hand turned sideways and the yo-yo parallel to the ground. Keep your elbow tucked near your side. This is a weird throw.

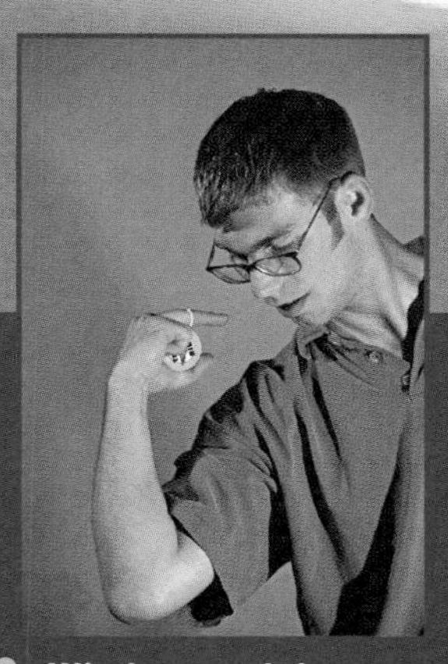

2. Wind up and throw across your body. Remember to keep your hand flat as the yo-yo leaves it. You want the yo-yo to sleep fast when it hits the end of the string.

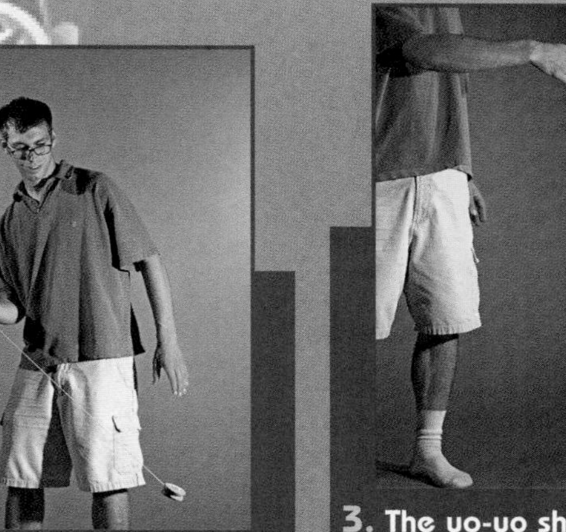

3. The yo-yo should hit bottom and start spinning sideways. UFO! The string will corkscrew wildly.

If you're a righty, throwing the UFO *away* from your body will tighten the string; if you're a lefty, the outside (away-from-the-body) UFO will loosen it. This effect is the opposite of an inside (across-your-body) UFO.

4. Hook the string with the thumb of your free hand. Push away from your body.

5. Raise your free hand until the spinning yo-yo is at shoulder height. Then quickly toss the yo-yo into the air and it will wind back down to your yo-yo hand. Area 51, watch out! You've just caught a UFO.

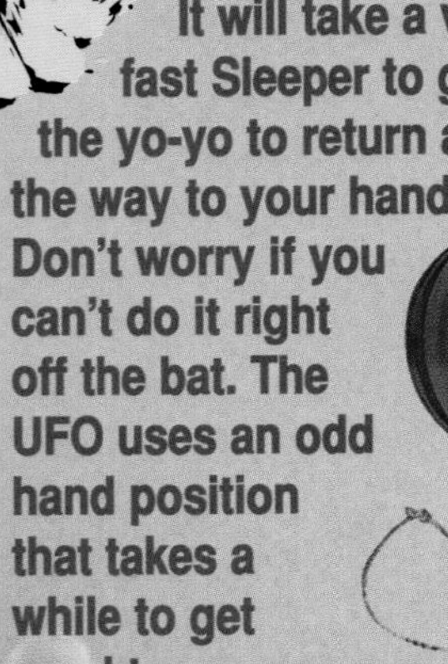

TIP It will take a very fast Sleeper to get the yo-yo to return all the way to your hand. Don't worry if you can't do it right off the bat. The UFO uses an odd hand position that takes a while to get used to.

Restart

Here's your chance to put the Basic Front Mount to the test. This is a satisfying move. Once again, it looks like the trick is over when you're about halfway into it. Then you surprise anyone watching. Read on and find out why.

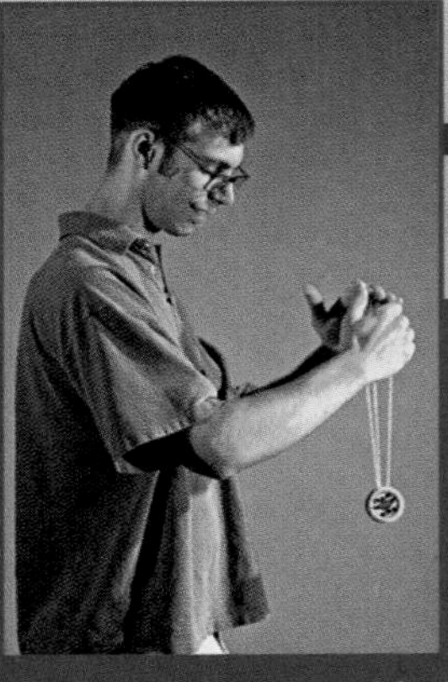

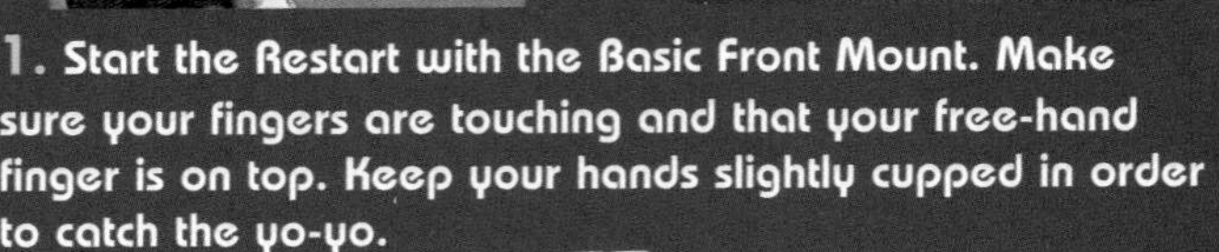

1. Start the Restart with the Basic Front Mount. Make sure your fingers are touching and that your free-hand finger is on top. Keep your hands slightly cupped in order to catch the yo-yo.

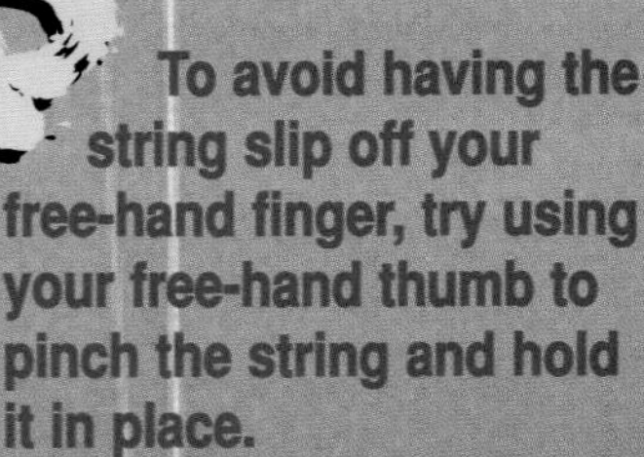

TIP To avoid having the string slip off your free-hand finger, try using your free-hand thumb to pinch the string and hold it in place.

2. Give a tug (sometimes it takes a few tries) and the yo-yo will climb the string into your cupped hands. Except for the little loop over your free finger and the yo-yo hand loop, all the string should be wound up inside the yo-yo.

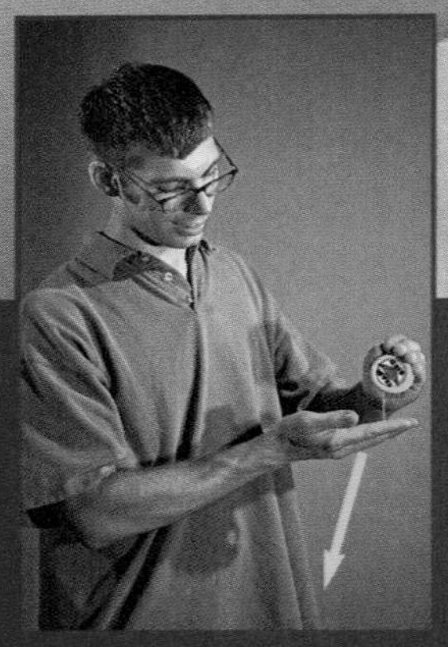

3. That's it, right? Wrong! With a smooth, fast motion, pull your yo-yo hand down and back. Keep your free hand very still so that the loop on it doesn't slip off.

4. Vroom! The yo-yo spins again. A perfect Restart.

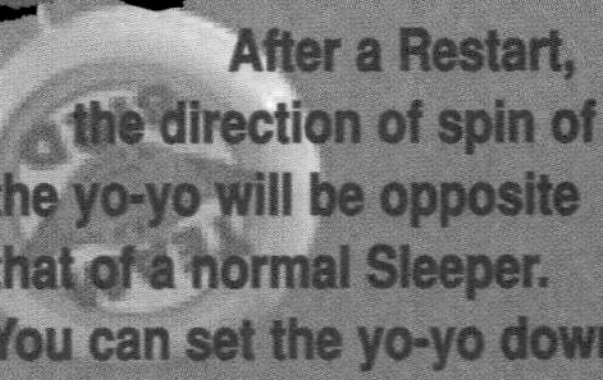

NOTE After a Restart, the direction of spin of the yo-yo will be opposite that of a normal Sleeper. You can set the yo-yo down and do a Walk the Cat.

Front Pinwheel

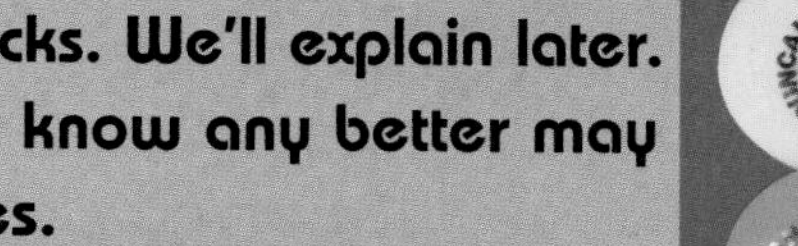

This trick is competition worthy because it's a stylish beginning to other tricks. We'll explain later.

The Front Pinwheel is actually harder than it looks. People who don't know any better may not be terribly impressed, but those of us who yo will know what it takes.

1. Back to something familiar. Throw a fast Sleeper. Hold the thumb of your free hand so the string is between your body and your thumb. Push your thumb against the string. Now pull your yo-yo hand down and your free hand up so the yo-yo rises. Leave about four to five inches of string between the yo-yo and the thumb.

Competition Tip

You can simply do this trick piece by piece. In competition, however, it must be one smooth motion. Use the momentum of the yo-yo as you raise it to flip it over your thumb and start the twirl. Not only is this competition standard, it's much more stylish.

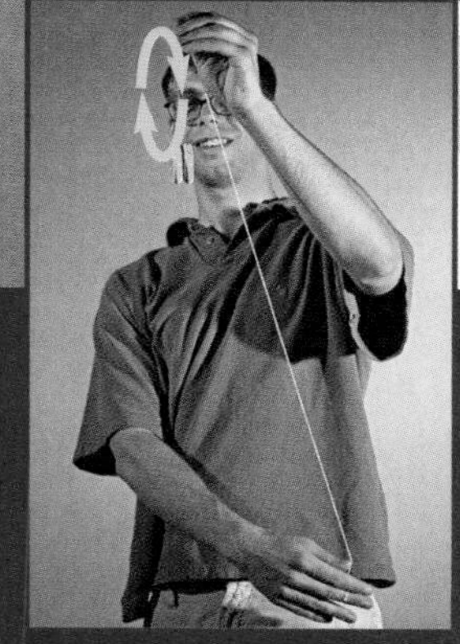

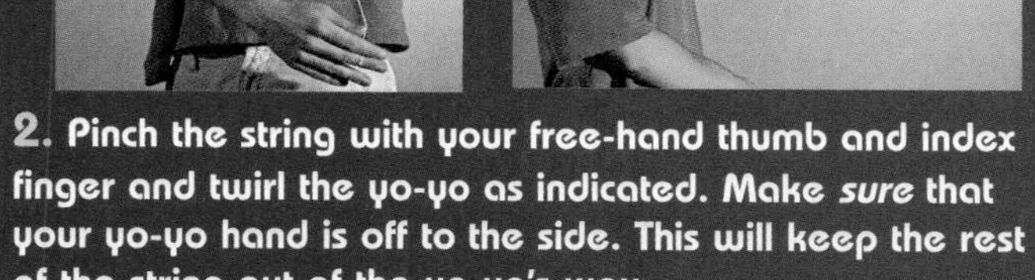

2. Pinch the string with your free-hand thumb and index finger and twirl the yo-yo as indicated. Make *sure* that your yo-yo hand is off to the side. This will keep the rest of the string out of the yo-yo's way.

3. Here you can see the regular end of the Front Pinwheel. Set the yo-yo down and then tug it to get it back to your hand. You can, however, use the Pinwheel to go on to other tricks. Use the momentum to do other string Mounts and Dismounts. Experiment.

Dog Bite and Pit Stop

These two tricks are good for a laugh and a quick stop. It's important to have on loose or baggy clothing while attempting either of these. Also, they're both very hard to do with a wing-shaped (butterfly) yo-yo.

First we'll cover the Dog Bite, then we'll go through the Pit Stop.

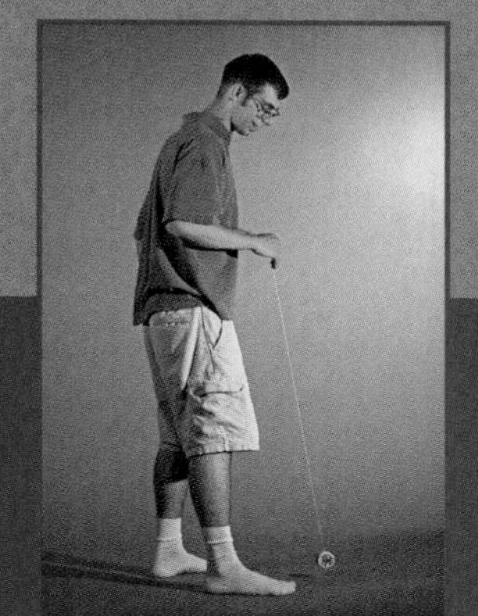

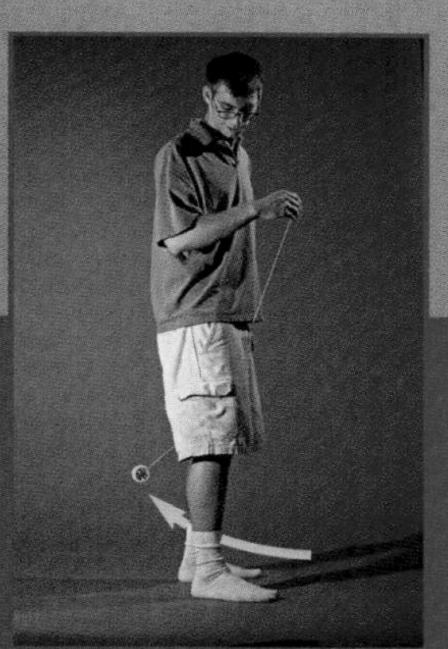

1. Throw a hard Sleeper. This time, instead of absorbing the swing, let the yo-yo swing between your legs.

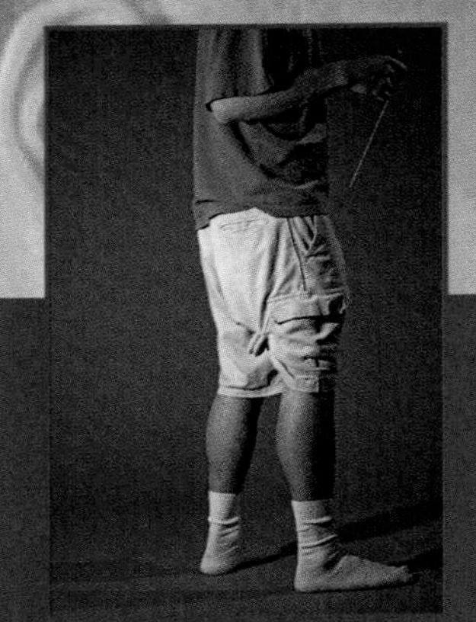

2. Give a tug and the yo-yo will start to return and then "bite" your pants (or shorts) and stick there. Don't worry, it doesn't hurt ... much.

3. The Pit Stop is very similar. Throw a Sleeper and let the yo-yo swing up between your arm and your body.

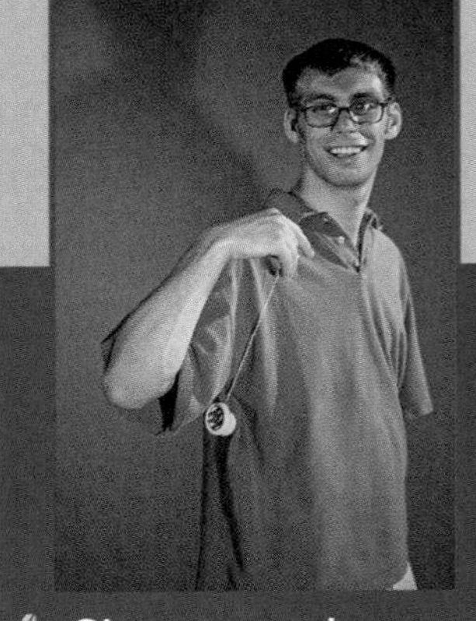

4. Give a tug and ... Whap! The yo-yo should catch just at your armpit. Hence the name, Pit Stop (duh).

YoYo CONTEST

Trivi-Yo

There are paintings of Napoleon's soldiers using yo-yos. Perhaps they were relaxing before a battle.

Texas Cowboy

Pull yourself up by your bootstraps and get ready for this variation of Around the World. You won't be able to rope a steer with this trick, but it will be fun to watch.

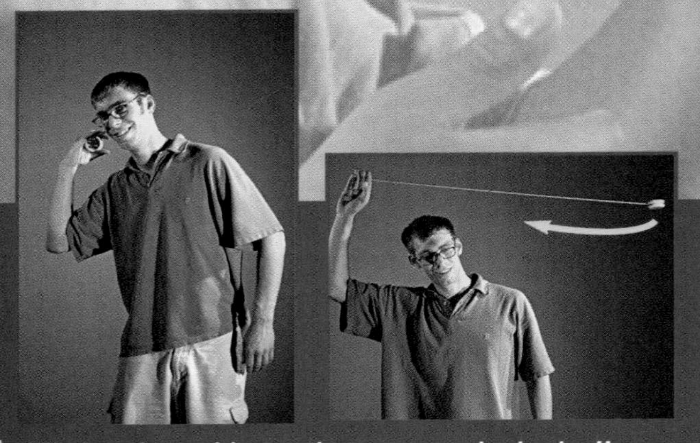

1. Wind up for a sidearm throw across the body. You want the yo-yo to sleep at the end of the throw.

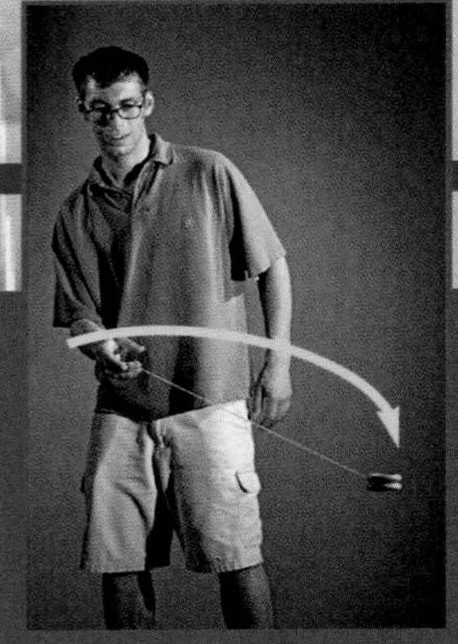

2. Swing the yo-yo over your head. This move is similar to a flat, high Around the World. Keep it going and sweep the yo-yo down as it travels across your body.

TIP Jump over the *string*, not the yo-yo. If you mess up and come down on the string, it isn't a problem, it's just embarrassing. If you come down too early on top of your yo-yo, well ... you probably needed a new one anyway.

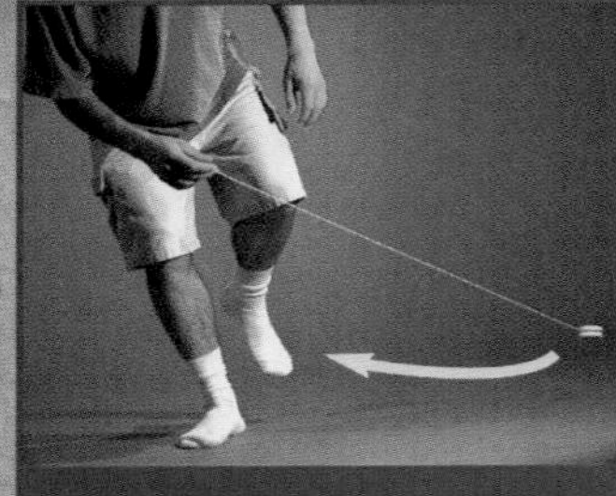

3. Bend and swing the yo-yo toward your feet. At the last second, jump!

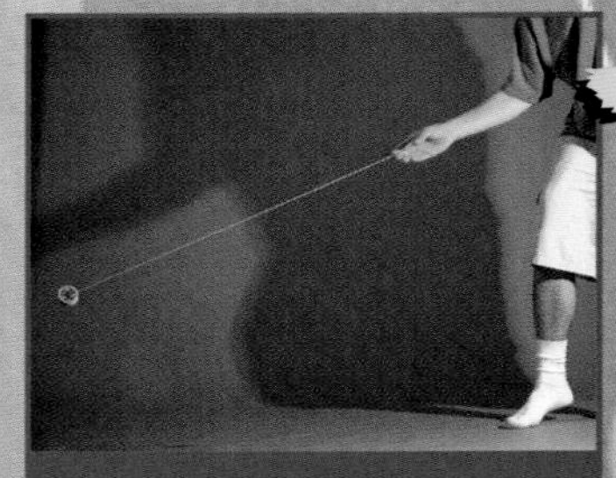

4. Finally, swing the yo-yo back up and return it to your hand. Yee-ha!

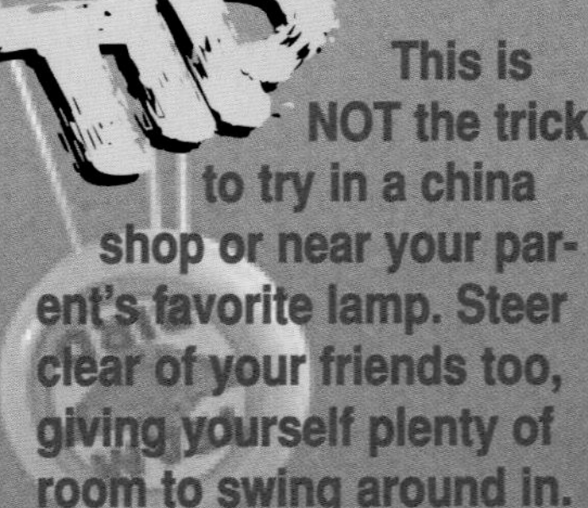

TIP This is NOT the trick to try in a china shop or near your parent's favorite lamp. Steer clear of your friends too, giving yourself plenty of room to swing around in.

Dizzy Baby

You've learned how to gently Rock the Baby to sleep. Now let's see whether you can give the Baby a ride! Dizzy Baby is a great trick because it's unexpected. People will see the set up and expect a regular Rock the Baby, then you throw in a change-up.

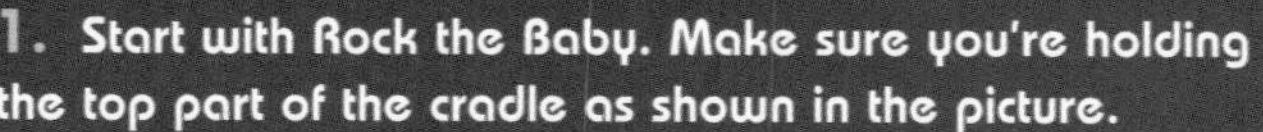

1. Start with Rock the Baby. Make sure you're holding the top part of the cradle as shown in the picture.

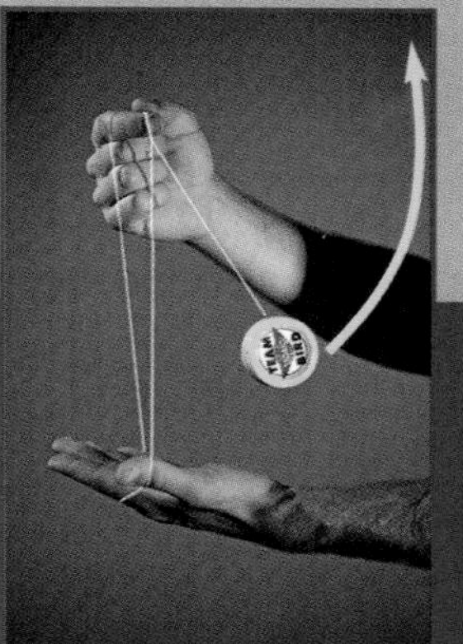

2. Now swing the yo-yo Baby *toward* your body and keep looping it.

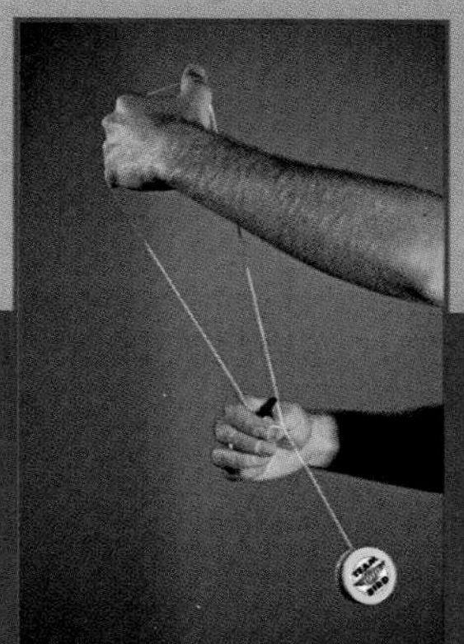

3. When Baby's had enough fun for one day, turn the cradle over and let the yo-yo drop. This will give the string time to unwind itself and prevent a nasty knot from forming.

Dizzy Baby *will* wind the string up at the top of the cradle. This won't stop the trick, but it does mean that you can't just do Dizzy Baby forever.

Tiny Baby

This is a second variation on Rock the Baby. This one proves that bigger isn't always better.

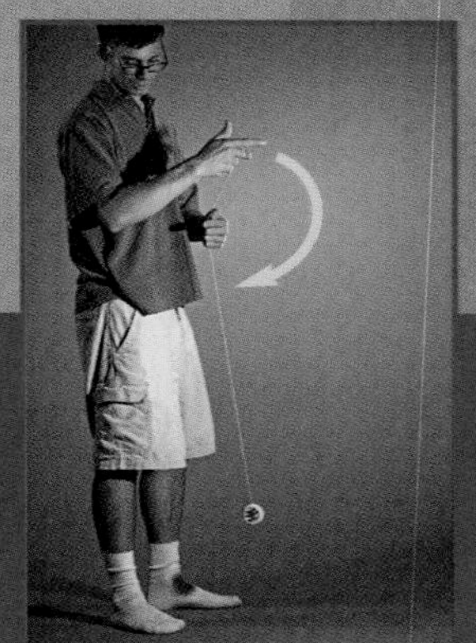

1. Throw a fast Sleeper and get ready for some string folding. Place your free-hand finger on the string so the string is between your body and the finger.

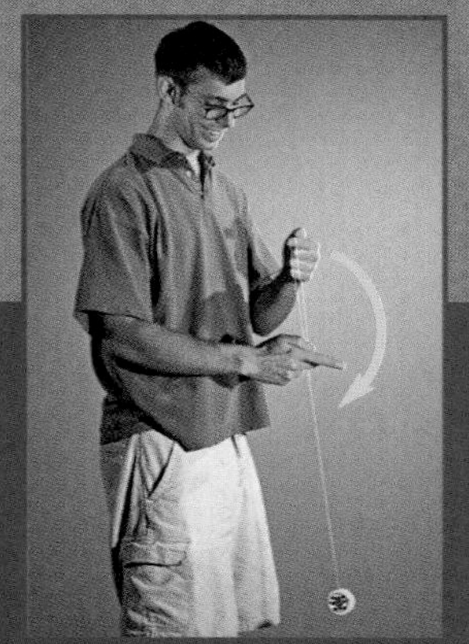

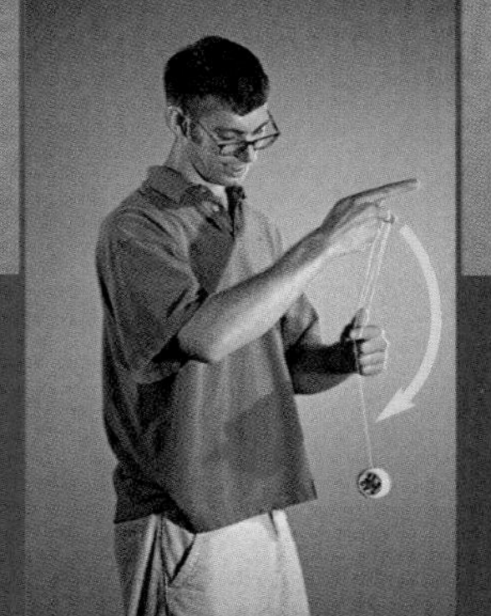

2. Bring your yo-yo hand over your free hand. Then bring your free hand over your yo-yo hand. And then (don't worry, last one) bring your yo-yo hand over your free hand. This should put your yo-yo hand about an inch or two from the yo-yo itself.

TIP Tiny Baby is a good trick to practice while your yo-yo is stopped. Doing a few dry runs will let you get the feel for the length of your string and where you need to make the multiple folds.

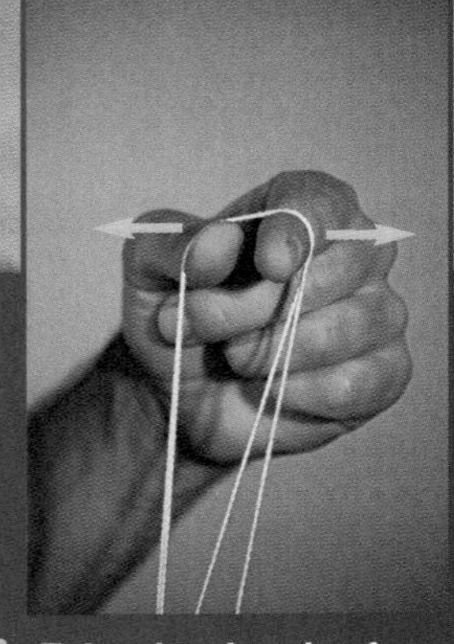

3. Take the thumb of your free hand and place it in the loop around your free-hand index finger. Spread the two fingers apart to form the triangle of the cradle.

TIP You may have to slide the string loops on your fingers to get them just right.

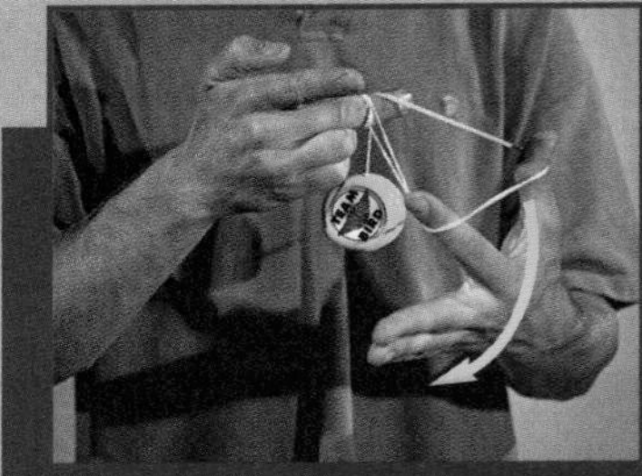

4. Bring the cradle down so it surrounds the yo-yo, and presto! Tiny Baby. Exit the trick by rewinding and doing the steps in reverse.

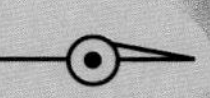

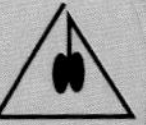

Trapeze Baby

It seems all right for a grown man to be on a trapeze, but a baby? Maybe it's the Man on the Flying Trapeze rocking his Baby? One way or the other, let's see how well the little fella can stay up there.

This is another Rock the Baby variation. There are many, but Trapeze Baby is the last one we'll show you. How many can you come up with?

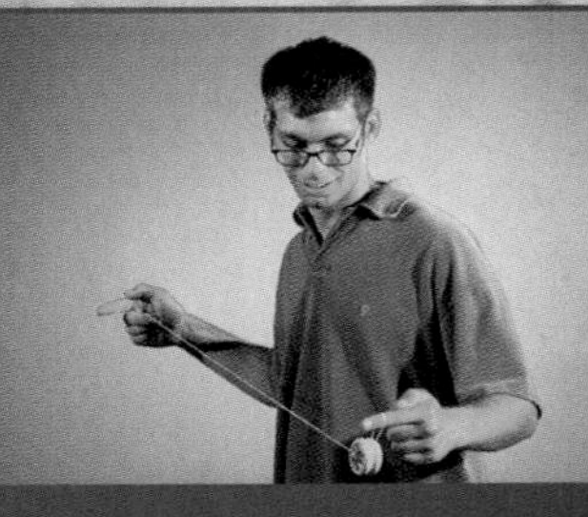

1. Start with the Man on the Flying Trapeze. Standard stuff that will show up again. We hope you know it by now.

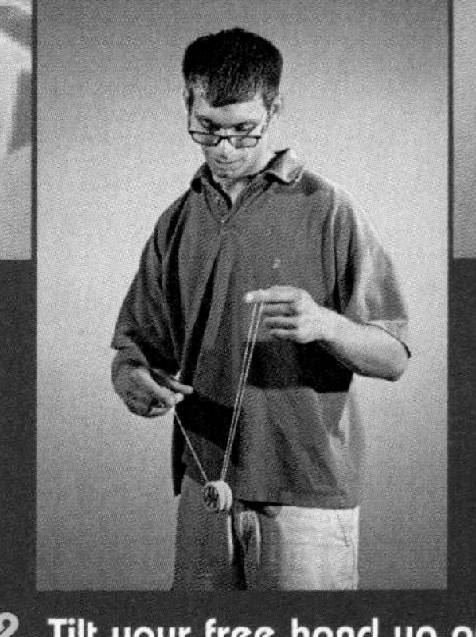

2. Tilt your free hand up and slide the yo-yo down so that it's closer to your yo-yo hand. With the thumb and index finger of your yo-yo hand, pinch all the string and hold tight.

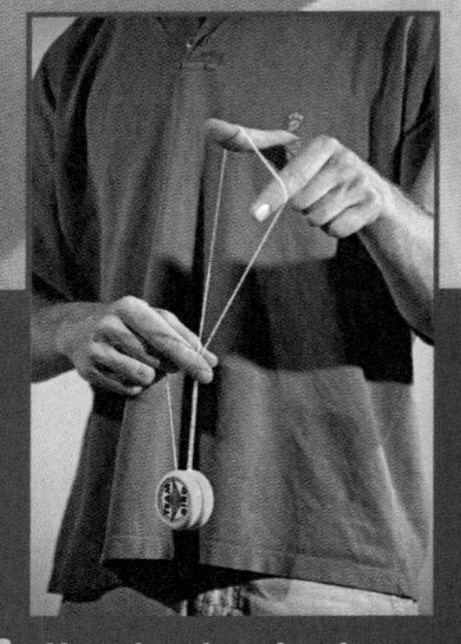

3. Use the thumb of your free hand to spread the string into a cradle. (Sound familiar? The Rock the Baby variations have many parts in common.)

4. Now turn the cradle over and rock that Trapeze Baby while it sleeps. To exit, simply rewind until you're back to the Man on the Flying Trapeze and then Dismount.

One-Handed Star

Trivi-Yo

Yo-yos can spin incredibly fast. A yo-yo can reach over 11,000 rotations per minute with a good, strong Sleeper.

Like the various Babies in the world of yo-yo tricks, there are also several Star tricks. We'll cover a few of them in this book, but we encourage you to come up with others. This is the basic One-Handed Star. It's complicated to describe, but we'll do our best.

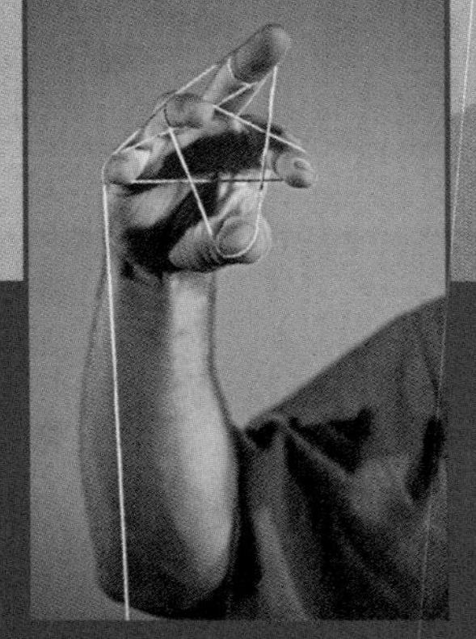

1. Here's the end result. We wanted you to see what you were working toward before breaking it down step by step.

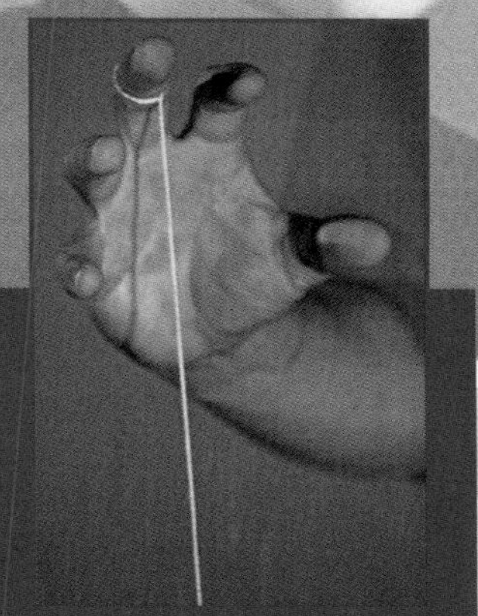

2. Start with a strong Sleeper. Hold your palm down and fingers spread wide.

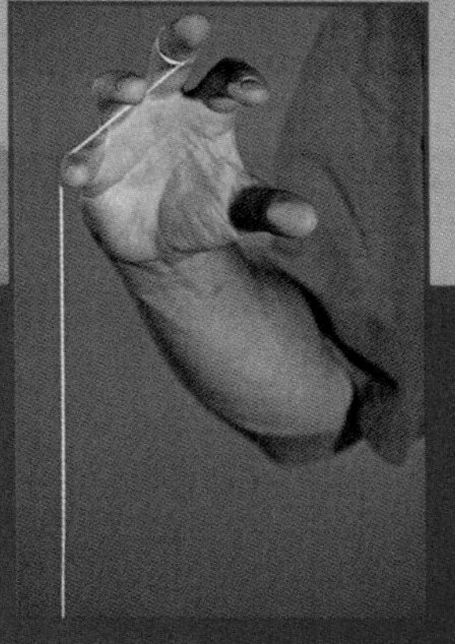

3. Now, without using your free hand, get the string over your pinkie.

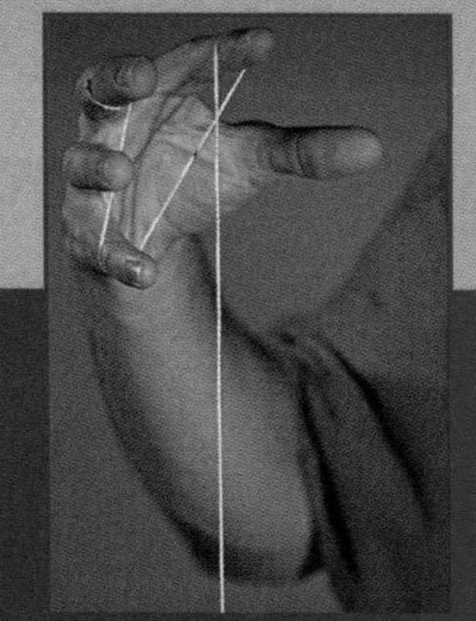

4. Tilt your hand and get the string over your index finger.

TIP Try to wrap the string high up your fingers. Too low and you'll get tied up.

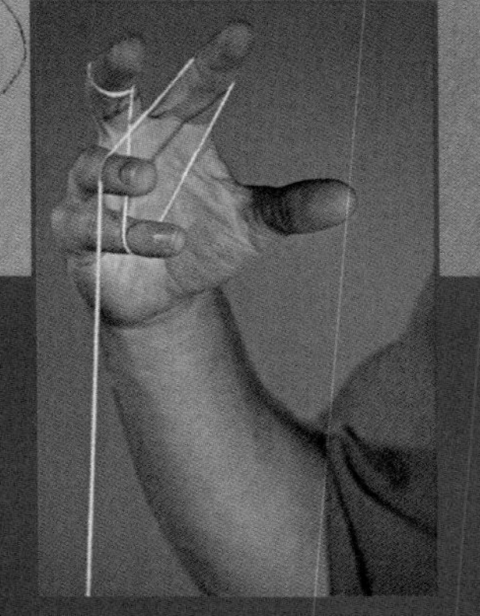

5. Now drape it over your ring finger.

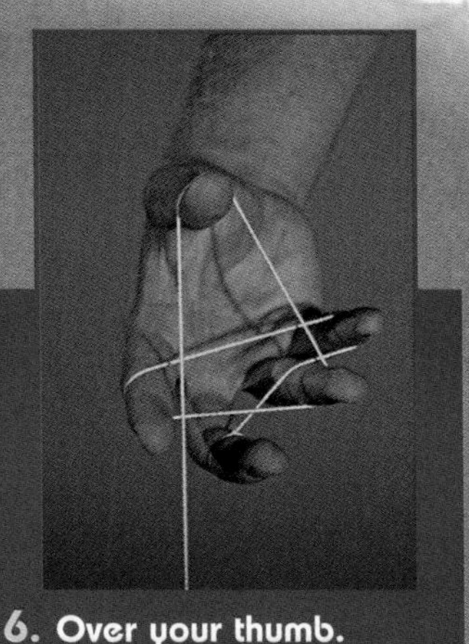

6. Over your thumb.

7. Once over the middle finger (make sure not to put the string over the index finger again). And there's your One-Handed Star.

8. To exit, tilt your hand down and bring your fingers closer together. The string should slide off and the yo-yo should pop back up!

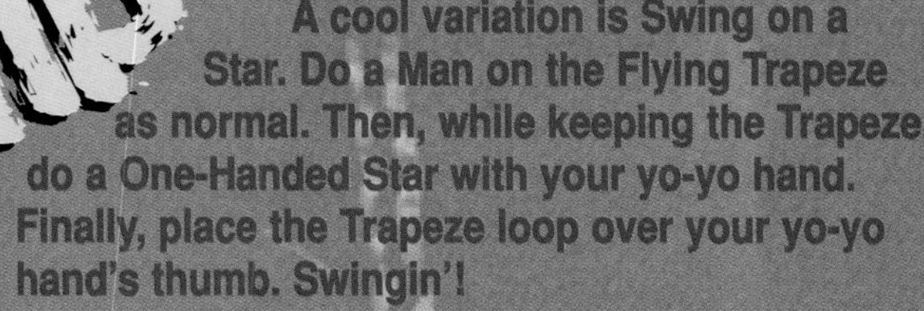

TIP A cool variation is Swing on a Star. Do a Man on the Flying Trapeze as normal. Then, while keeping the Trapeze, do a One-Handed Star with your yo-yo hand. Finally, place the Trapeze loop over your yo-yo hand's thumb. Swingin'!

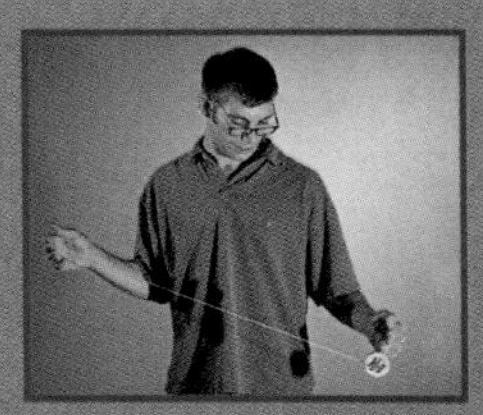

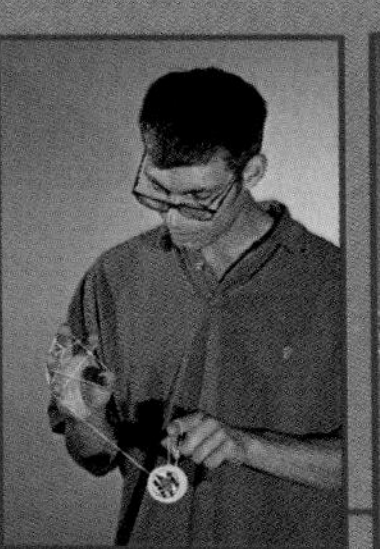

Eiffel Tower

To accomplish this string-pattern trick, all the yo-yo needs is a fast Sleeper. You, however, have to be able to make shapes with the string. Not so easy. Read on and find out how to help your yo-yo see a little bit of French culture.

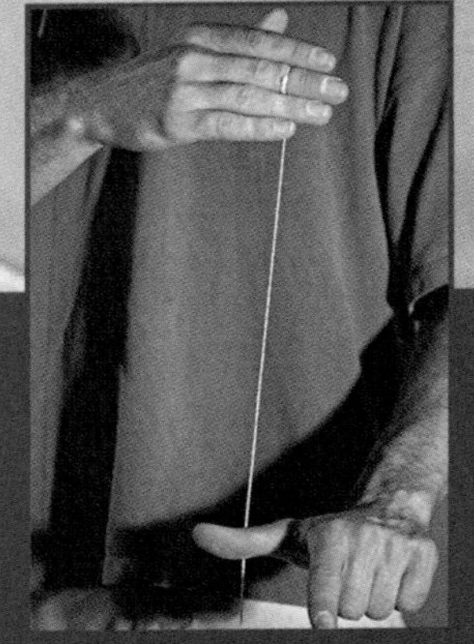

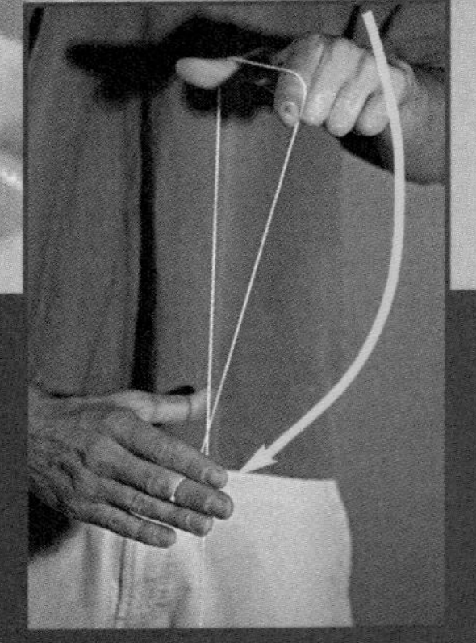

1. Throw a fast Sleeper. Make an L with the thumb and index finger of your free hand. Loop the string over that L. Make sure you're draping the string *away* from your body.

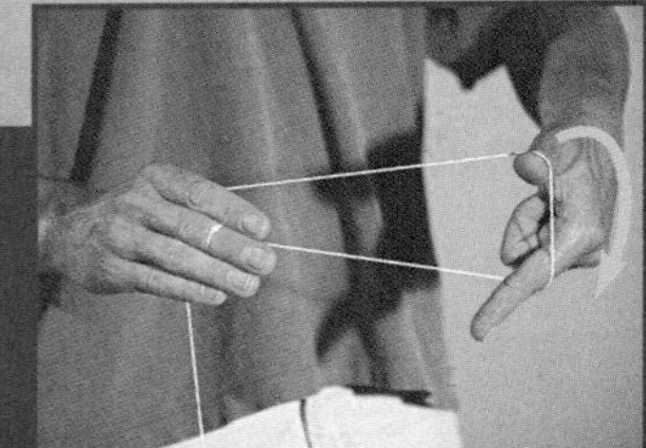

2. Hook the string with the thumb of your yo-yo hand. Catch it in the web of your thumb and hang on. Then twist your free hand away from your body to make an hourglass shape in the string.

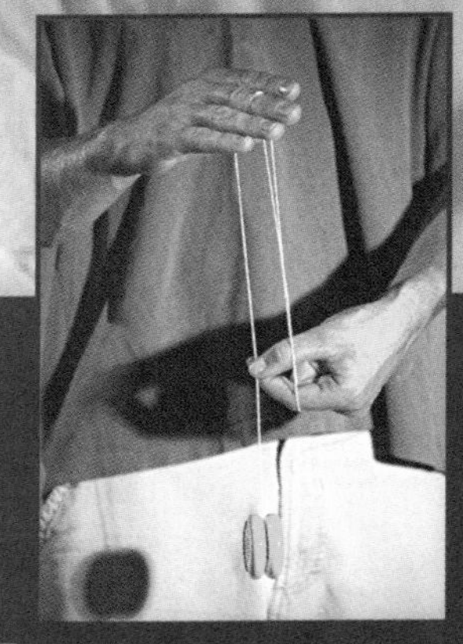

3. Pinch the string above the yo-yo with the index finger and thumb of your free hand.

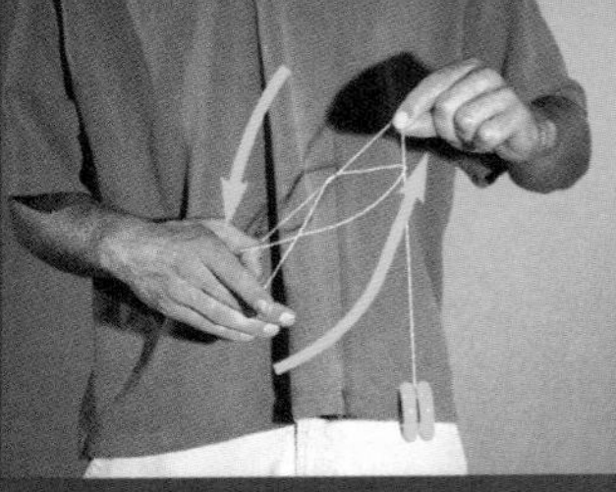

4. Pull the string pinched in your free hand and bring it up. Remember to keep the string hooked over the thumb of your yo-yo hand. (Confused yet? So are we. But carry on, we're almost there.)

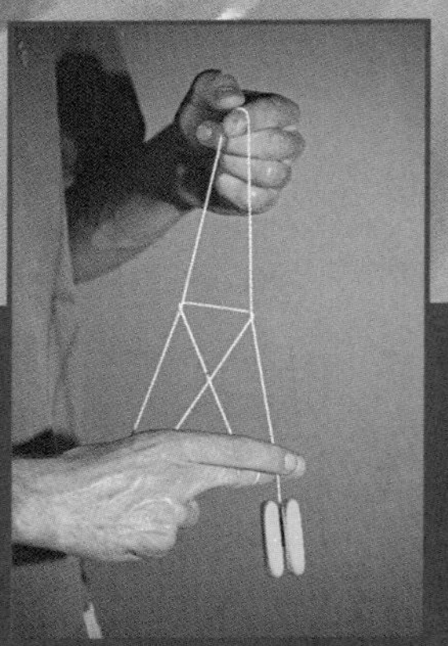

5. Now, pull up on the string pinched in your free hand. Let the yo-yo's weight help drape the string over your yo-yo finger. Voila! The Eiffel Tower. *Tres magnifique*!

TIP Do not be too frustrated if this doesn't come out right on your first try. The Eiffel Tower is a good trick for you to practice with a dead yo-yo before trying to do it full speed.

Yo Maneuver

This is a single- or two-person trick, but we suggest that you try it with two people. If you ever have the chance to perform with another person for an audience, then you must know this trick. Trust us, the audience will love it.

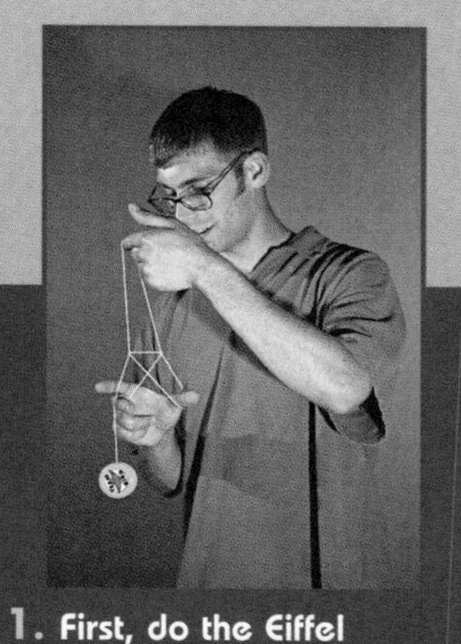

1. First, do the Eiffel Tower. See above for details on that trick.

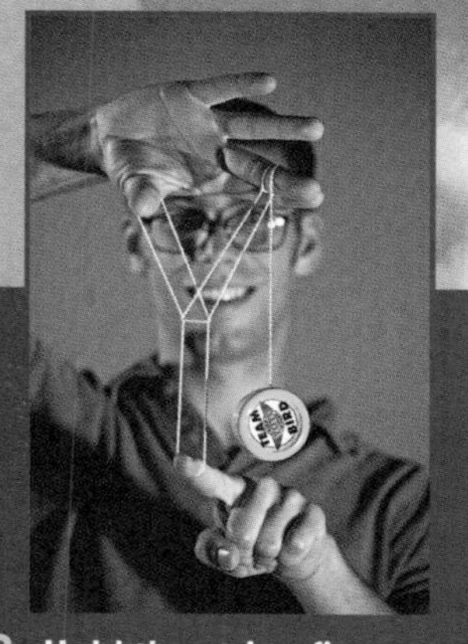

2. Hold the string figure tight and turn it over so that the string is a Y and the yo-yo is an O. You have just spelled "Yo."

3. Get a buddy to help you out and you can spell "Yo-Yo." What better way to end, or begin, a performance? You can let the audience know what they just saw or what they are going to see.

TIP Do you think you might be able to Rock the Baby through the bottom of the Y?

Brain Twister

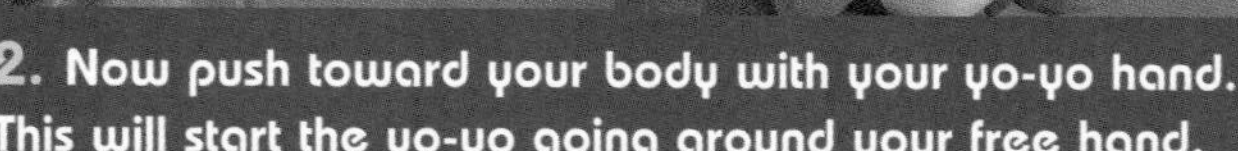

Here we go. This is a famous trick and one that still impresses at least one of the authors of this book. It looks good and feels great when you pull it off for the first time. And the second. And the third ...

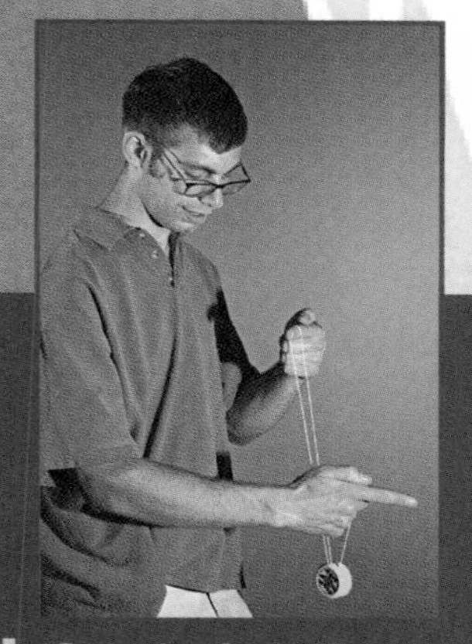

1. Start the Brain Twister with the relatively easy Basic Front Mount. This time, however, let your yo-yo hand come to about halfway up the string.

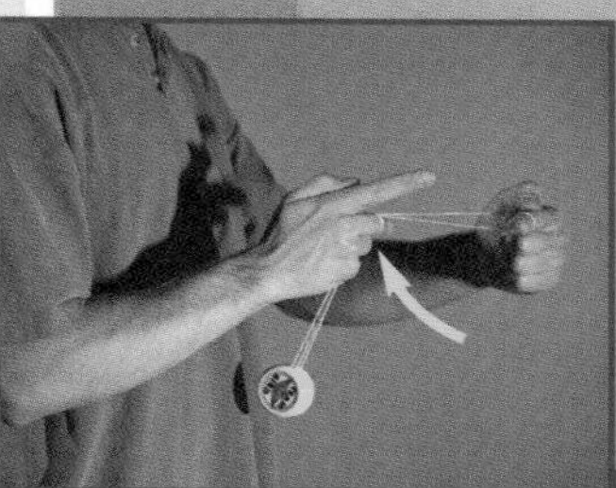

2. Now push toward your body with your yo-yo hand. This will start the yo-yo going around your free hand.

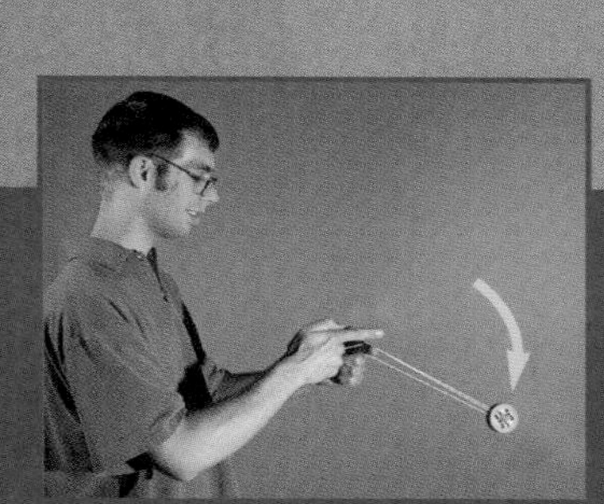

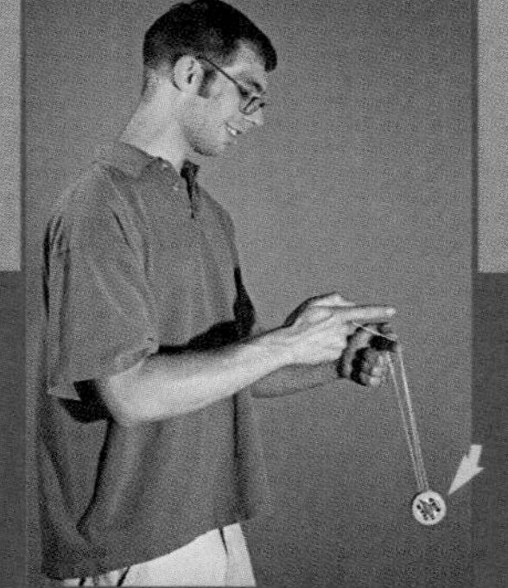

3. Let the yo-yo go around in a full circle so it ends up back in the Basic Front Mount position.

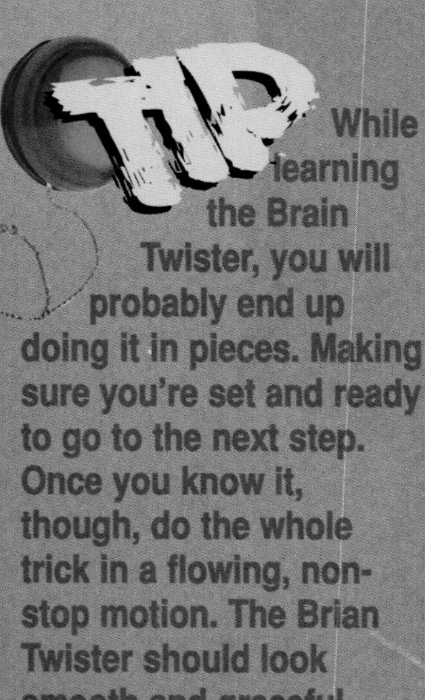

TIP While learning the Brain Twister, you will probably end up doing it in pieces. Making sure you're set and ready to go to the next step. Once you know it, though, do the whole trick in a flowing, non-stop motion. The Brian Twister should look smooth and graceful.

Competition Tip

You can just let the yo-yo return without sending it into a Loop. But only when you're just playing around. If you're in a competition you must end the Brain Twister with a Loop. In fact, most of the tricks from here on need to be ended with a Loop in competition.

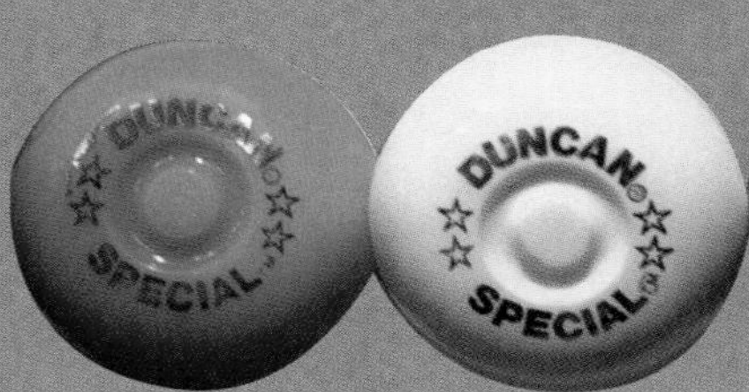

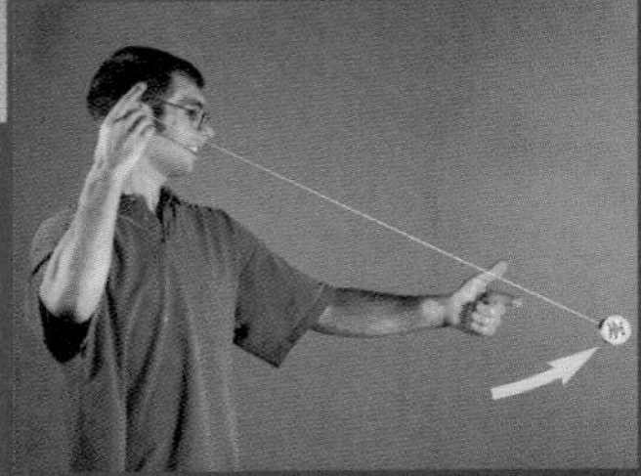

4. Dismount as you normally would for the Basic Front Mount. This time, however, don't just let the yo-yo return to your hand. Let it come back, and then ...

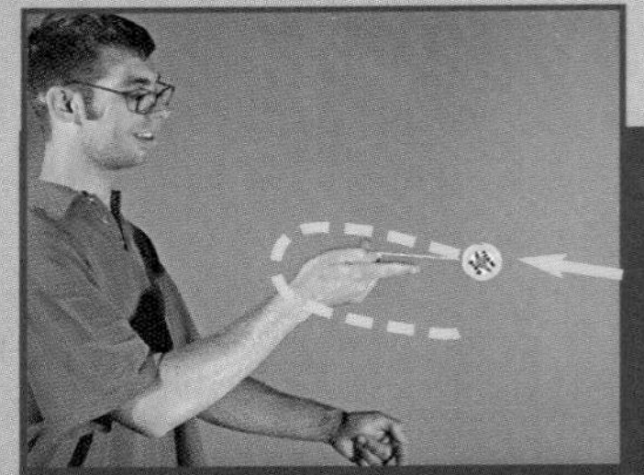
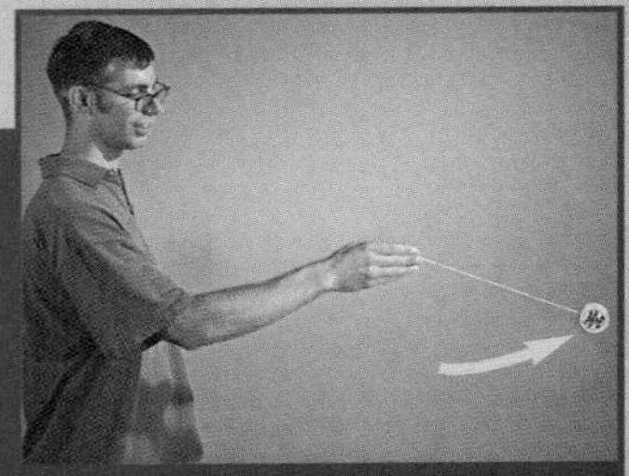

5. Loop it! Guide the yo-yo over your hand and out in a Loop. *Then* let it return, knowing that you've done a competition-worthy Brain Twister.

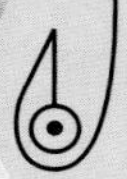

Quick Draw

This here trick is known by a few names, but we're partial to the Quick Draw. Some folks call it Mini Around the World, or Gunslinger (that ain't so bad), but we're Quick Draw artists. This ain't no ride on the ranch, so listen up, pardners.

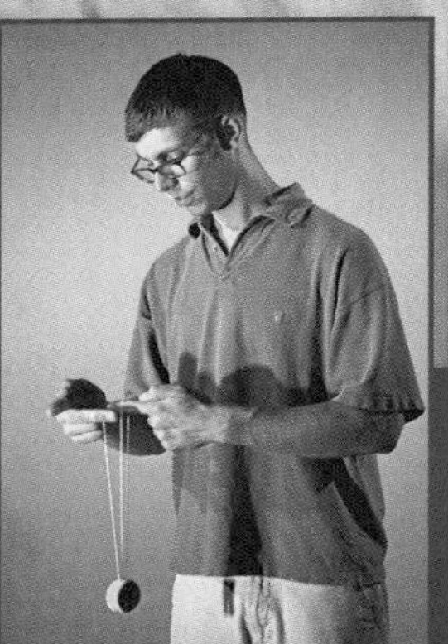

1. All right. Start with the Front Mount (y'all have mastered this by now, right?). Take the loop of string that's on your free-hand index finger and place it gently on your yo-yo string finger.

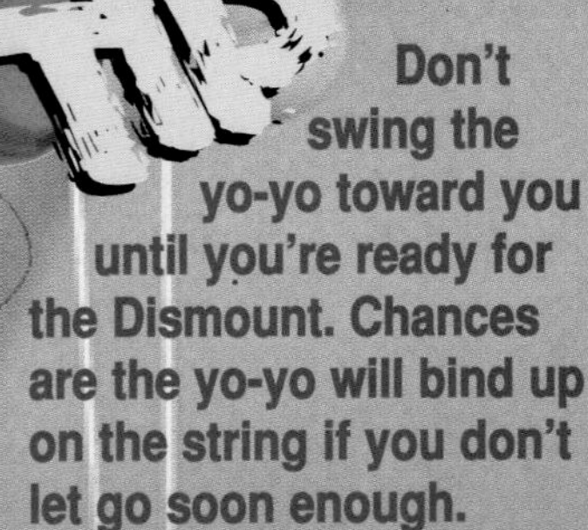

TIP Don't swing the yo-yo toward you until you're ready for the Dismount. Chances are the yo-yo will bind up on the string if you don't let go soon enough.

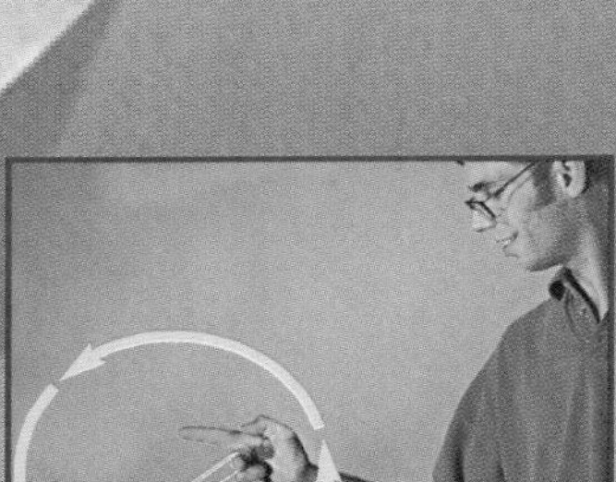

2. Start swinging the yo-yo in a circle away from your body. The longer your yo-yo sleeps, the more circles you can make.

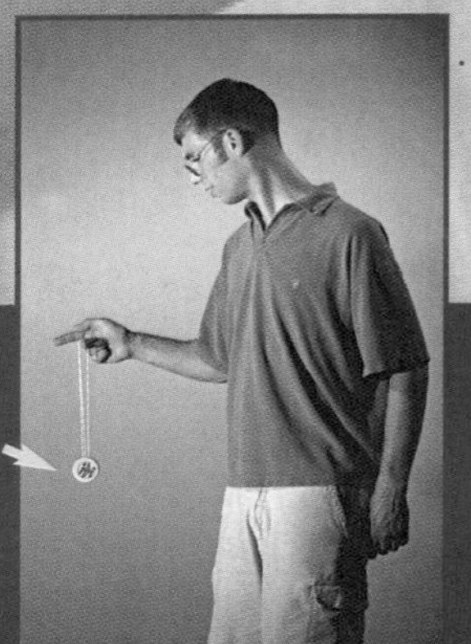
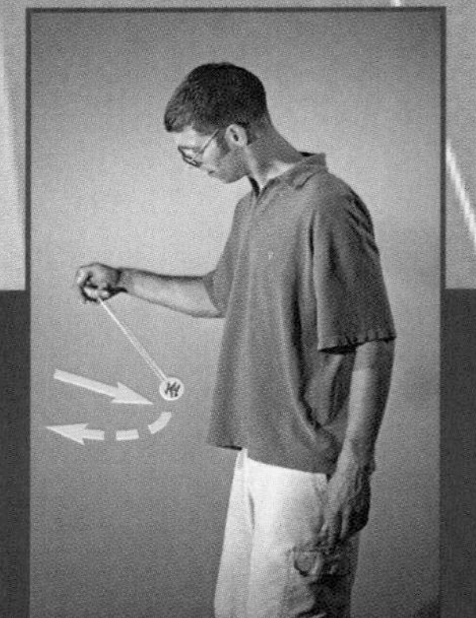
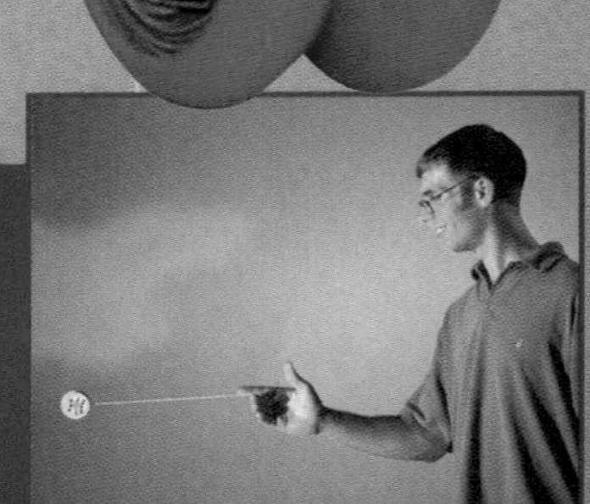

3. When you know it's time to stop showing off your Quick Draw, stop the circles. Reverse the direction of the yo-yo, swinging it toward your body. Do this only once, though, letting go as soon as you can get the yo-yo to go out into a Forward Pass. It'll return to your holster and you can mosey into the sunset.

30 Loops

This isn't a trick. It's a goal. Loops are important in yo-yoing for fun and in competition yo-yoing. They show up all over the place, in trick after trick, but they can be very hard to master.

We figure that if you can do three perfect Loops then there's no reason why you can't do 10. And if you can do 10 perfect Loops, you can do 30.

Here are some tips and tidbits to help you reach the goal stated above: 30 Loops.

The "control angle"

- If you lose control of your Loops, stop! Catch the yo-yo and try again. Flailing with your hand while you try to recover won't help.

Perfect Loop form

- Start small, build small. Keep count of how many you can do in a row. Then try to break your record by just one Loop. Keep building on that and soon you'll be up into double digits.
- Strive for perfect form and control. No corkscrewing string, no Loops that go wild. Just Loops as even and regular as a heartbeat.
- Remember that a perfect Loop does *not* mean that the yo-yo is perpendicular to the ground. The yo-yo will be tilted slightly out. This is called the "control angle."
- Three words (again): Practice, practice, practice. But if you're getting too frustrated, stop! Walk around, take a deep breath, eat a snack, then go back and try again. Forcing yourself to go on when you're angry will not do any good.

10 Opposite-Hand Loops

You've done 30 Loops. You can get perfect Loops and talk at the same time. But can you do Loops with your *off hand*?

You heard us. Can you righties do left-handed Loops? Can you lefties do right-handed Loops?

No? Well, now's the time to learn. There's nothing new to be said about them except—do them with your other hand!

You may need a lot of practice to pull off Opposite-Hand Loops. The payoff will be worth it. Once you master Loops with one hand and then the other, you get to move on to *Two-Handed Tricks*! Using two yo-yos at the same time.

Sound impossible? We have a section in this book with pictures to prove it's for real.

First, though, you must be able to do Opposite-Hand Loops. The same advice applies. If you can do three, you can do five. If you can do five, you can get to 10

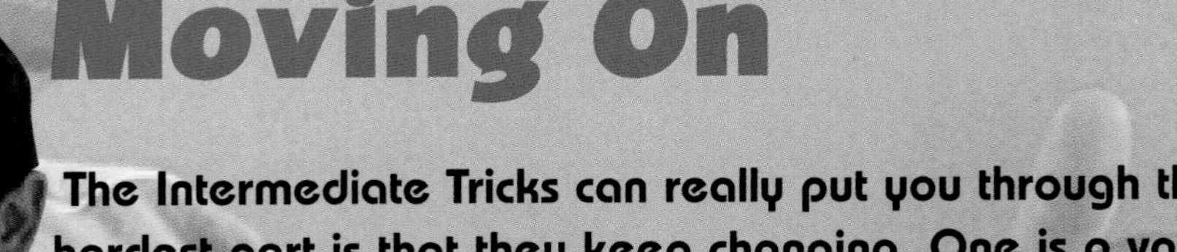

Moving On

The Intermediate Tricks can really put you through the paces. The hardest part is that they keep changing. One is a variation of Rock the Baby, the next is a Mount, and the next is a string grab.

By now you should be thinking of ways to combine the tricks with smooth transitions. We'll give some advice in the later chapters on combining tricks, but freestyling is all about your creativity and skill. You know what works best for you.

Also, spend some time fixing the rough edges and trouble in your tricks. Don't assume that doing a Texas Cowboy successfully once means that you know the trick. You know what works for you and you know what doesn't work. Fix what's broken and then read on! The Advanced Building Blocks await you!

Advanced Building Blocks

Get Ready for the Big Time!

If you don't own a transaxle yo-yo, then put this book down and go buy one before you read further.

We're not saying that you *can't* do these Building Blocks with a fixed axle. Who knows, you might be that good (or you might be able to throw a *really* fast Sleeper). A transaxle yo-yo will most likely save you a ton of frustration, though. The Mounts in this section, the largest Building Block section in the book, require a yo-yo to sleep for *at least* 10 seconds. Longer than that is even better!

So, with your transaxle in hand, read carefully and study the pictures. Plus, keep reminding yourself that this is only the advanced *Building Block* section. These Building Blocks may seem like tricks (and most of them are, actually), but you'll need them to build up a truly impressive arsenal of advanced tricks.

Building Blocks

Front Mounts

This is a small collection of Mounts that bring you to rest in the Front Mount position. They are all useful and will come up again, so don't think they're just fancy ways of doing a Basic Front Mount.

Note

Take this time to review the Basic Front Mount in the Intermediate Building Blocks section. It will figure heavily into many of the tricks that follow.

Under Mount

The Under Mount fools many yo-ers. It doesn't require as much effort as most people put into it. You may have some trouble trying to force the yo-yo around, but as you learn, start smoothing it out. In the end, it should seem as though the yo-yo simply hops up without any effort from you at all. Check it out.

1. Start with a *fast* Sleeper. Hold your yo-yo hand high (not as high as you can—you'll need to lift it in a second). Stick out the index finger of your free hand about four inches from the yo-yo. Position it so that your free hand is between your body and the string. Then press your free-hand index finger against the string enough to dent the string out a bit.

2. Here's the tricky part. Lift your yo-yo hand up. This motion will cause the yo-yo to flick up and around your free-hand index finger. Catch the yo-yo on the string ...

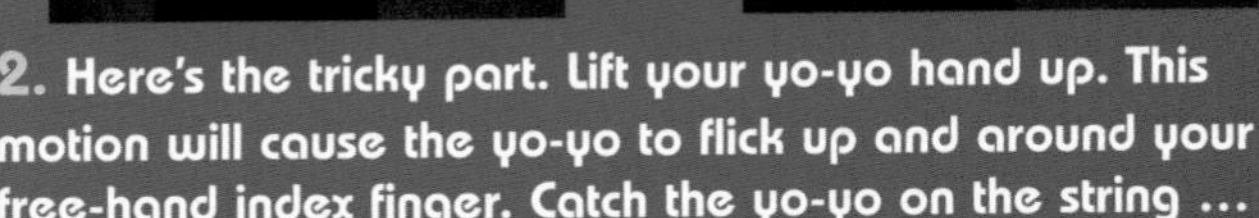

TIP The part that fools people is that you don't need to move your free-hand index finger *at all* to get the yo-yo onto the string. Once you've dented the string out, keep that free hand still. The motion of your yo-yo hand pulling up and then down will loop the yo-yo over your free hand. Trust us.

3. Then quickly lower your yo-yo hand. The yo-yo will sag down onto the extra string. There you have your Under Mount!

TIP Guess what? If you've done the Under Mount correctly, the yo-yo will be in the exact same position as when you've done the Basic Front Mount! The Under Mount is a different path to the same place. Don't be mad, though: you'll need the Under Mount a little later.

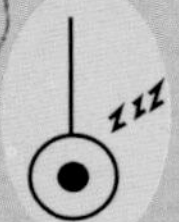

Over Mount

Another Mount that gets you into the same position as the Basic Front Mount. This one has some snappy style to it. You need to know your Front Pinwheel for this one, so if you're rusty, now is the time to review.

Competition Tip

For extra style points, do three Front Pinwheels with the yo-yo and *then* catch it on the string. Keen!

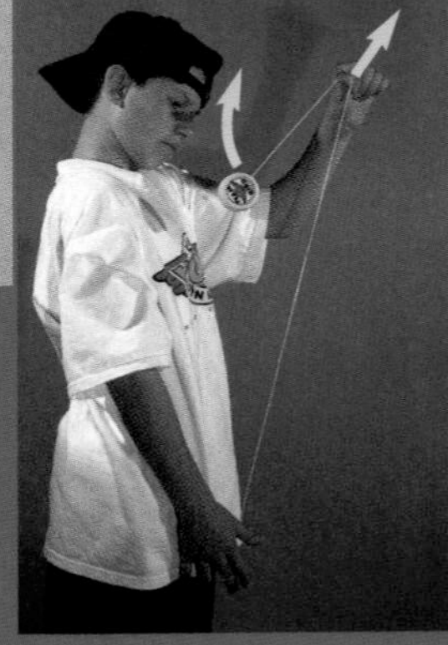

1. Start as you would for a Pinwheel. Do a hard Sleeper, then drape the string over your free-hand thumb. Push up with your free hand.

2. Push that thumb up and then pinch with the index finger of your free hand. Tug the yo-yo over the index finger and catch it on the string.

3. Let the yo-yo slide down into the Front Mount position. From here, you can do whatever your twisted brain (hint) desires.

Over-Under Mount

This is also known as the "Split Mount" and, believe it or not, you already know the parts of this neat Mount. There's an easy way of doing the Over-Under Mount that we will cover in detail. Then there are some variations that we'll touch on at the end.

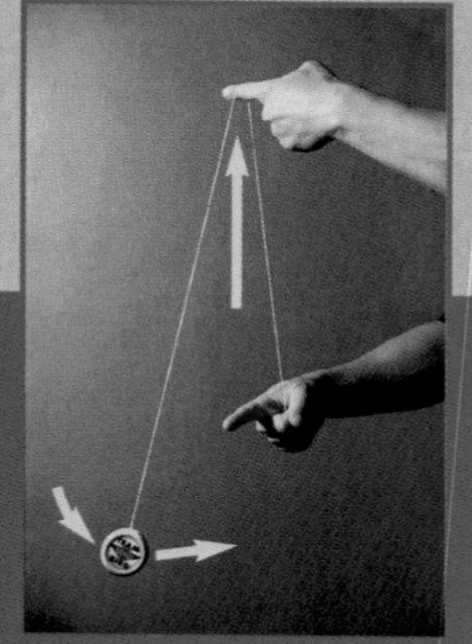

1. Start with a fast Sleeper (naturally) and begin as you would for a Basic Front Mount. Drape the string over the index finger of your free hand and pull it back and down.

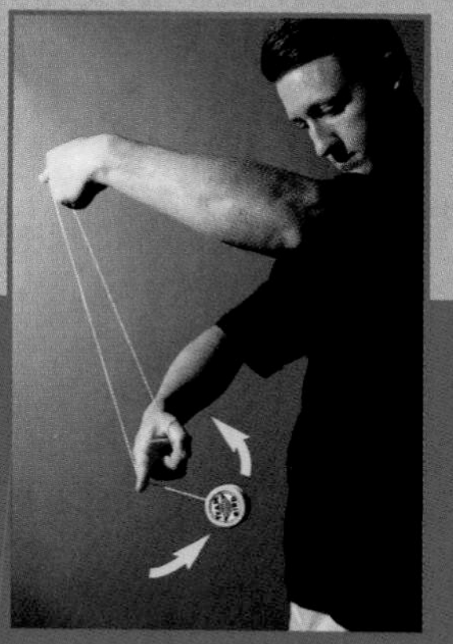

2. Bring the string close to your yo-yo hand, but keep the yo-yo *below* that yo-yo hand. Curl your string finger in and stick out the index finger of your yo-yo hand.

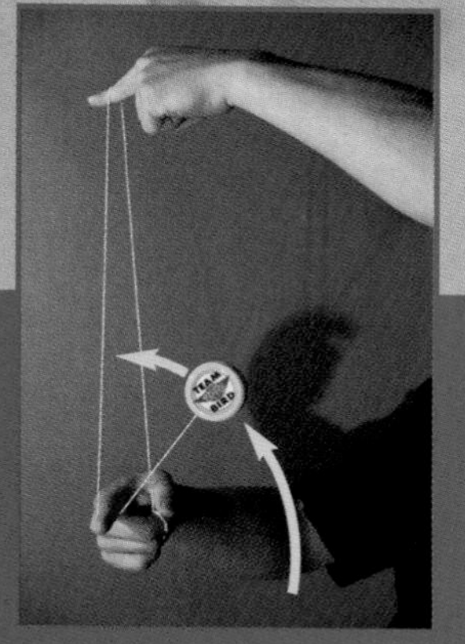

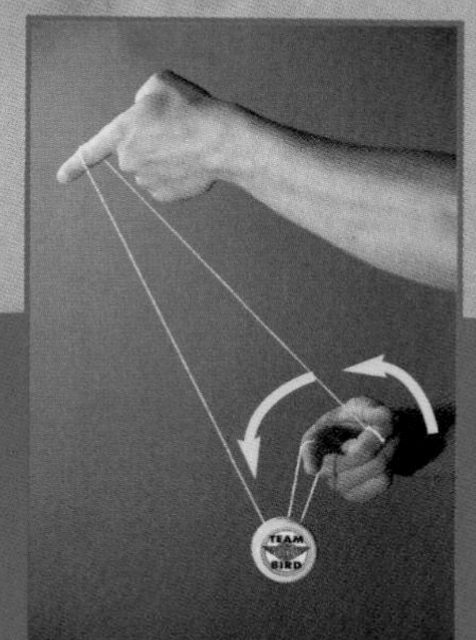

3. Now do a small Under Mount to get the yo-yo onto the string.

Over-Under Mount Variations

Here are some other ways to complete the Over-Under Mount.

From the Over Mount

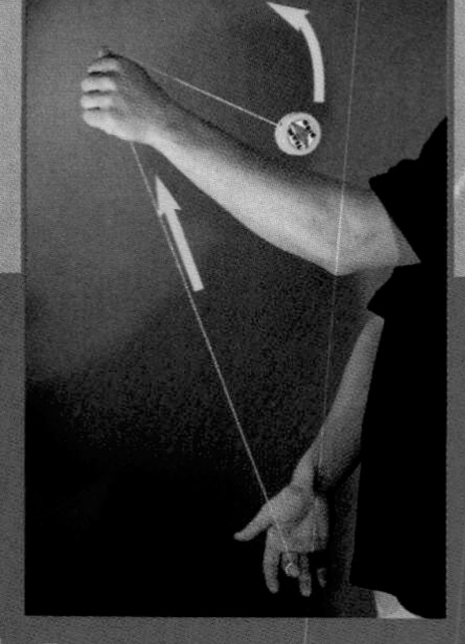

1. Start as you would for an Over Mount. Push the string up with your thumb.

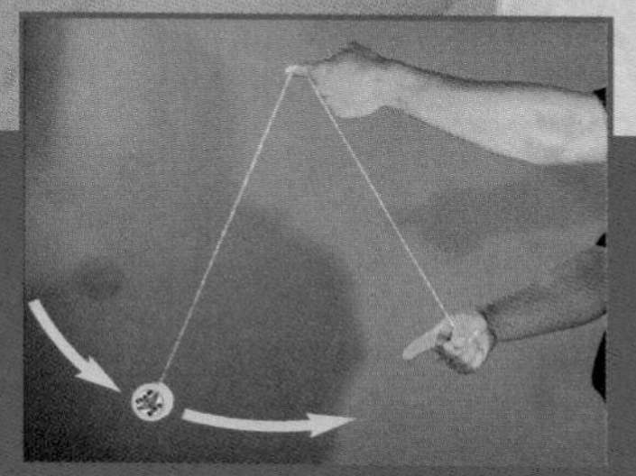

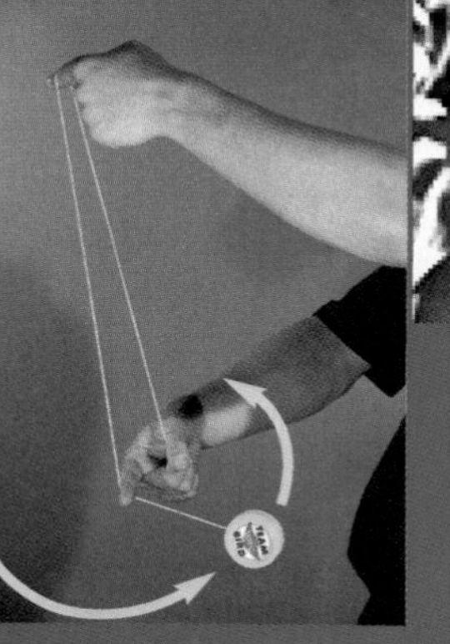

2. Flick the yo-yo over your free-hand index finger as you would for an Over Mount. This time, however, let the yo-yo travel out a bit, sliding the string with it. Guide it to swing under the index finger of your yo-yo hand.

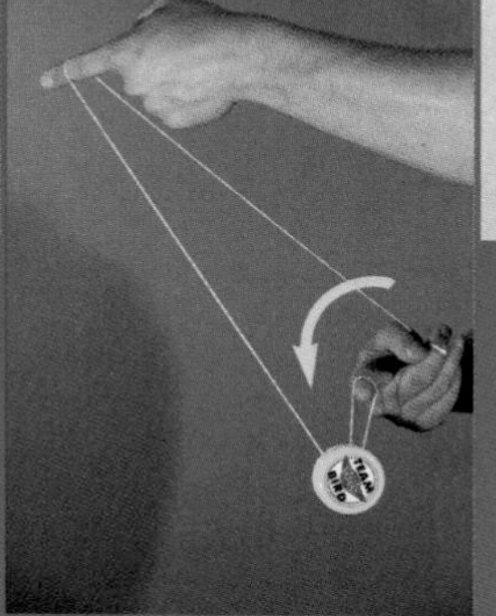

3. And then guide it into a small Under Mount. Ta-daaa!

From the Pinwheel

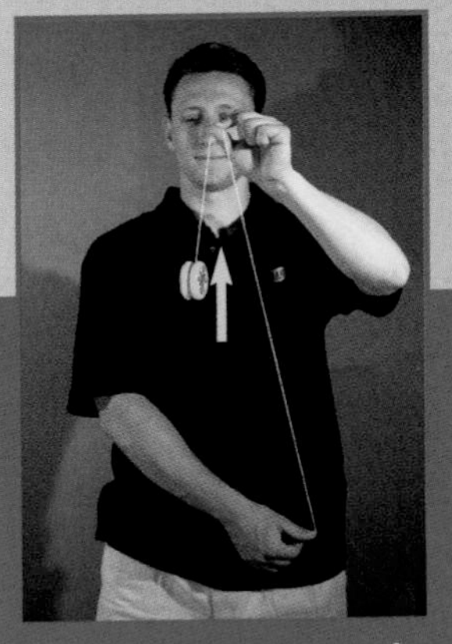

1. This is the same as the variation starting from the Over Mount except that when you reach the point shown here ...

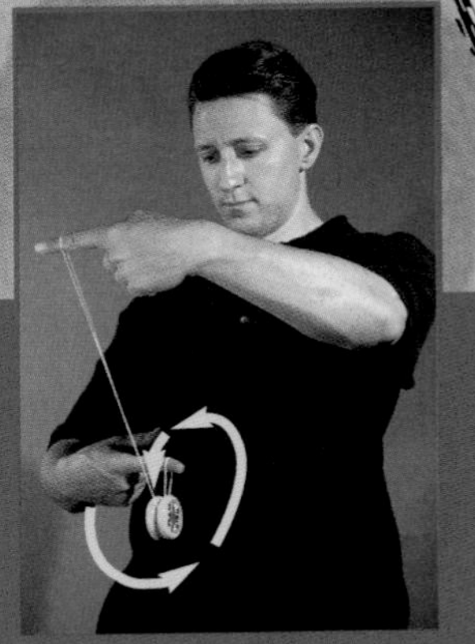

2. Do at least three Pinwheels before completing the Mount (complete it just the way you did from the Over Mount).

TIP When the yo-yo fires off in front of you, your free-hand index finger will have a double loop of string on it. When you lower your yo-yo hand (see next step), pinch the *inner loop* (the one farthest from the tip of your finger) with your thumb. Then slip the outer loop off. Seems complicated, but you should get the hang of it.

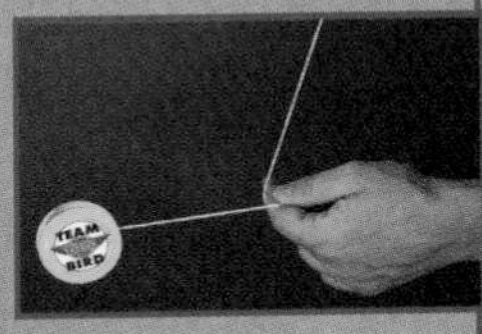

Shotgun

This variation is dynamic. It's fast and very cool. It's also tricky, so pay close attention.

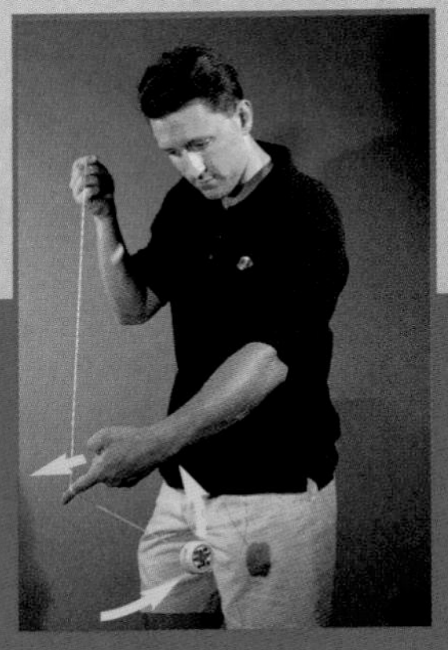

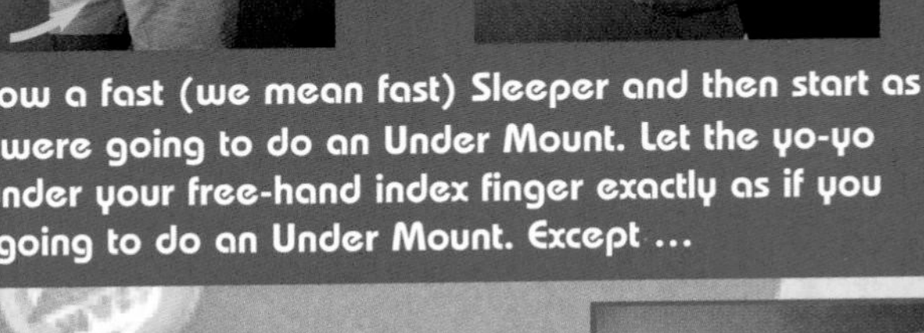

1. Throw a fast (we mean fast) Sleeper and then start as if you were going to do an Under Mount. Let the yo-yo loop under your free-hand index finger exactly as if you were going to do an Under Mount. Except ...

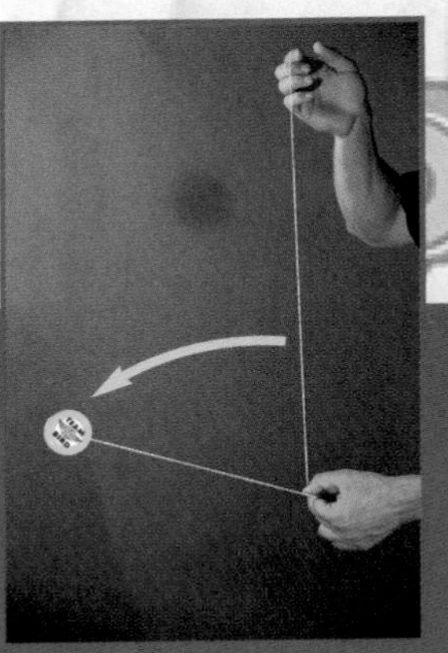

2. Intentionally *miss* the string with the yo-yo. Let the yo-yo shoot out, straight away from your body. At the same time, lower your yo-yo hand to let the string slide out with the yo-yo.

Trivi-Yo

Yo-yos can spin incredibly fast. A yo-yo can reach more than 11,000 rotations per minute with a good, strong Sleeper.

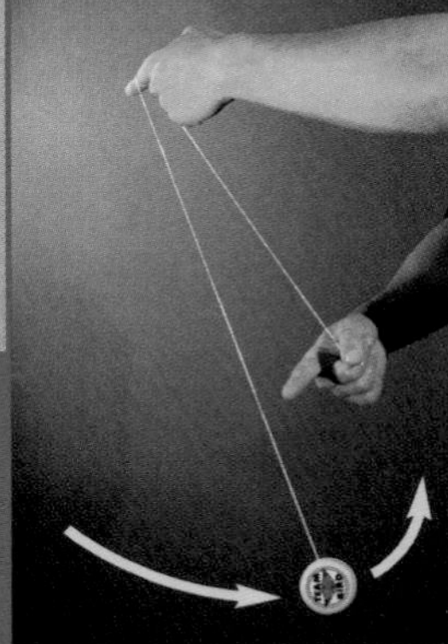

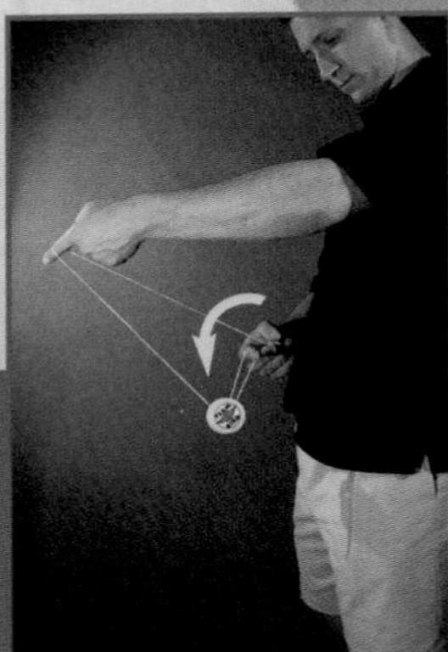

3. Get your yo-yo hand below your free hand and stick out the index finger. From here out, it's a normal Over-Under Mount.

Roller Coaster Mount 

This is one of the hardest Mounts you'll learn. The Roller Coaster Mount (also know as the One-and-a-Half Mount) is a sideways maneuver that will give your audience a good view. It's also a fun Mount, the completion of which requires a combination of yo-yo momentum and hand motion.

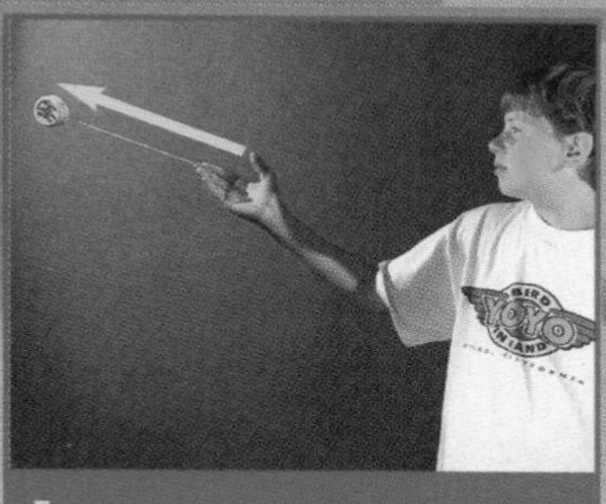

1. This Mount starts with a Break Away. In fact, the first parts should be very familiar by now.

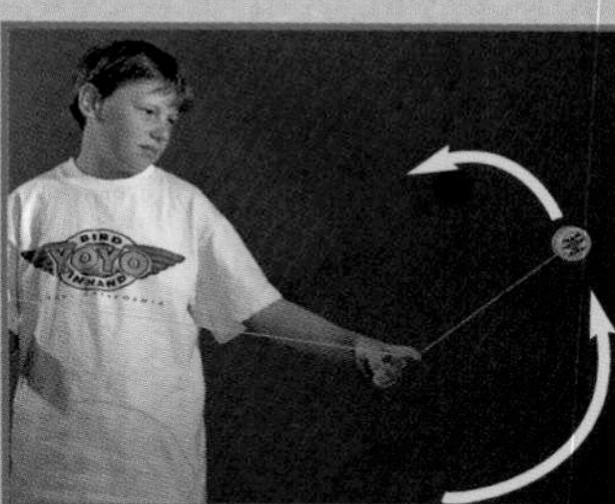

2. What's this? Seems like a Man on the Flying Trapeze. Familiar and (by now) easy, right? There is a catch, however. Once the yo-yo is curling over that index finger ...

3. Lift your free hand so it is directly above your yo-yo hand. *At the same time*, lift your yo-yo hand up to let the string slide over your free hand. The yo-yo should end up below your yo-yo hand.

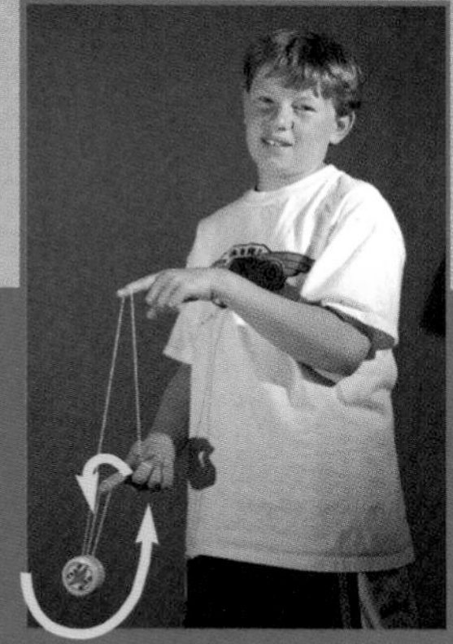

4. Now perform an Under Mount with that yo-yo-hand index finger. Catch the yo-yo on the string, and you've just finished the Roller Coaster Mount!

TIP To exit the Roller Coaster, simply pull your hands apart and let the yo-yo pop off the string. You can then swing it around for more sideways tricks for a really wild ride.

 Hydrogen Bomb Mount 

You might want to think of this Mount as a backward Over-Under Mount. The Hydrogen Bomb Mount involves yo-yo momentum, hand motion, and *body* movement. No worries, though. You'll come to love it.

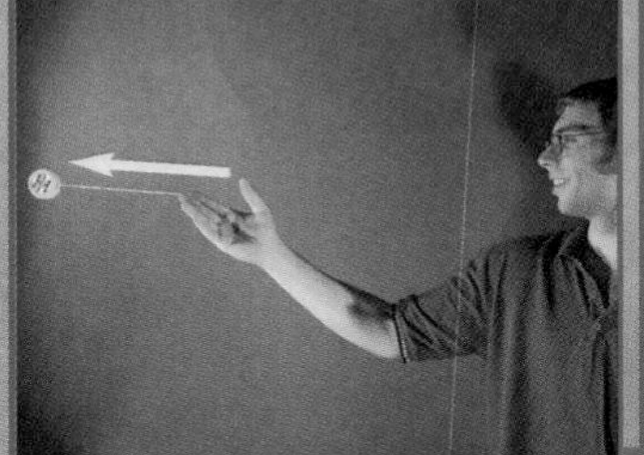

1. Start with the Break Away, good and fast. Then pretend like you're going to do a Man on the Flying Trapeze. But, instead of catching the yo-yo on the string ...

2. Let the yo-yo miss the string so that it hangs *between* your body and the string across your fingers.

3. This takes a little coordination. Bring your free hand up and your yo-yo hand down and forward. This will let the yo-yo slide lower. At the *same time*, turn your body 90 degrees to the left (to the right if you're left-handed) so you're facing the yo-yo.

4. Stick out that yo-yo-hand index finger and let the yo-yo loop over it (like a backward Under Mount).

5. The end result should look like this. The Hydrogen Bomb Mount. Remember it well—you'll see it again.

TIP To Dismount, simply pull your hands apart. Be careful as the yo-yo comes around your free hand. It has a tendency to get close to your face.

Double or Nothing

This sideways trick is a hoot. Once you've got it down cold, you can slide it into just about any combination with a sideways set of tricks. Double or Nothing builds from the basic Man on the Flying Trapeze motions and takes them one step further. Take a peek.

1. Start with a Break Away and go into a fake Man on the Flying Trapeze. Keep your hands *much* closer than you would for a real Man on the Flying Trapeze—you'll need a lot of extra string.

2. Let the yo-yo arc over both hands and wrap over your yo-yo finger. But don't stop there.

3. Keep it going around the free-hand finger again. Then finish as you would with a Man on the Flying Trapeze by catching the yo-yo on the *outermost* string.

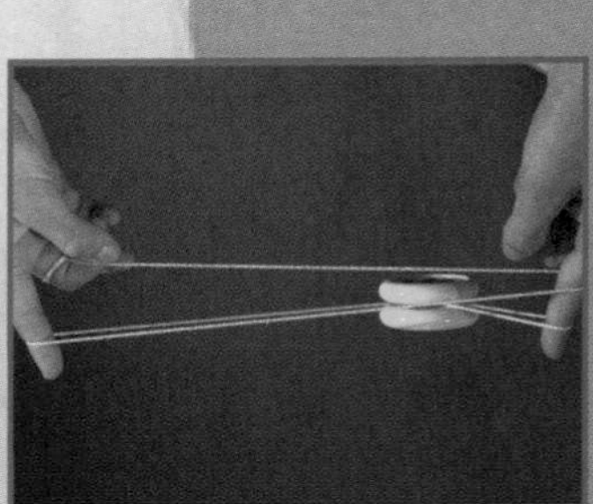

4. This is the outermost string. If you miss it, you'll know why this trick is called Double or *Nothing*.

TIP Make sure that the first turn of string stays far back on your fingers. This will keep it out of the way of the string on which you catch the yo-yo. And that will make your life much easier.

Double or Nothing: Dismount

The "Or Nothing" family of tricks includes a few Dismounts. Most basic is a Fly Away, just as for the Man on the Flying Trapeze. A fancier one is the Roll-Out Dismount, shown here.

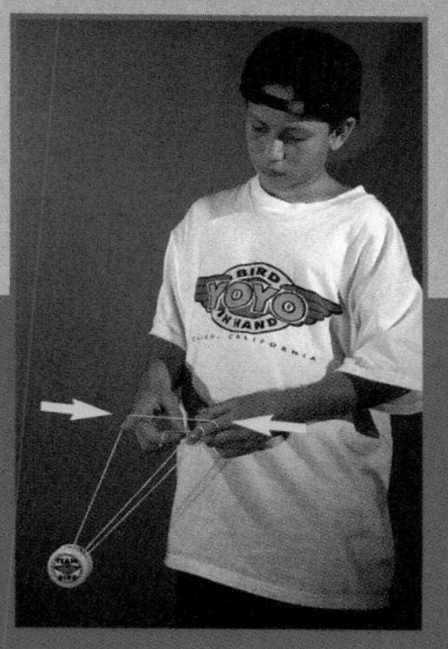

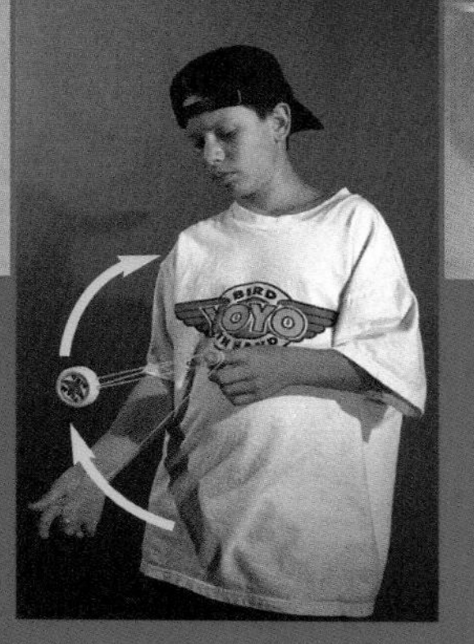

1. From Double or Nothing, slide the string off the index finger of your *yo-yo hand*. This will leave all the loops on your free hand.

2. Gently pull your hands apart. The yo-yo should unwind itself over your free-hand index finger and into (ta-da!) the Man on the Flying Trapeze. From there, do a Fly Away. Or you can do some Somersaults and Backflips (covered later), Rock the Baby, etc., to perform a really neat transition.

Competition Tip

For extra style points, give the yo-yo a gentle swing for the Roll-Out Dismount. Use the momentum to get the yo-yo over your free-hand index finger and slide the loop off your yo-yo hand. This method looks very smooth when done correctly.

Triple or Nothing

Did you think that Double or Nothing was tough? You don't know tough. Try Triple or Nothing for tough. Almost the same as Double or Nothing, Triple or Nothing adds another trip around your fingers before landing the yo-yo on the string. You may need a smaller yo-yo.

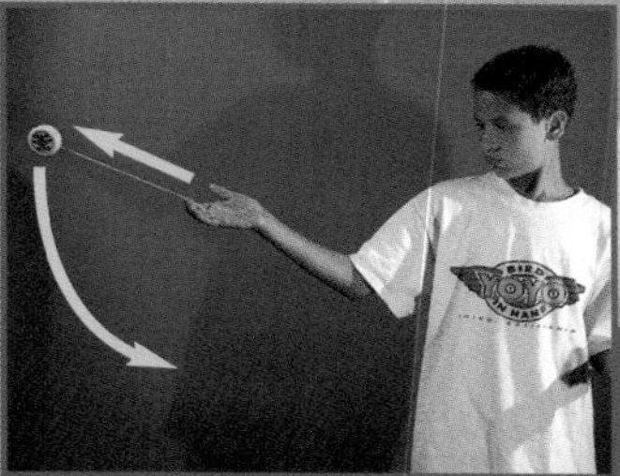

1. Do what you did for Double or Nothing. This time, however, keep your hands closer together and don't land the yo-yo after the second time around the free hand.

TIP You *can* Roll Out from the Triple or Nothing. Same type of action as for the Double. Slip the loops off your yo-yo-hand index finger and then the yo-yo must spin over your free-hand index finger *twice* to get to Man on the Flying Trapeze.

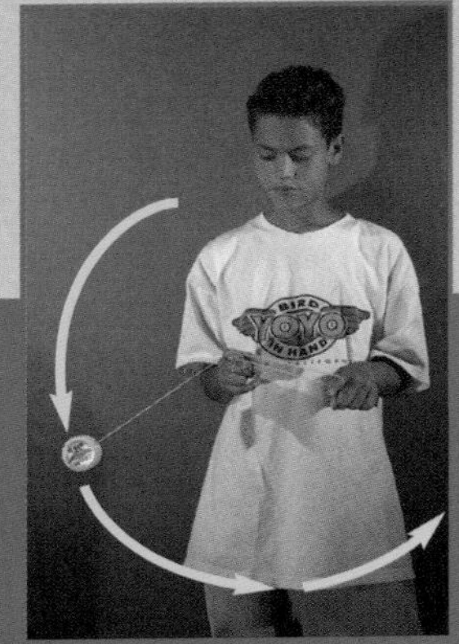

2. Keep going! Back over that yo-yo-hand index finger.

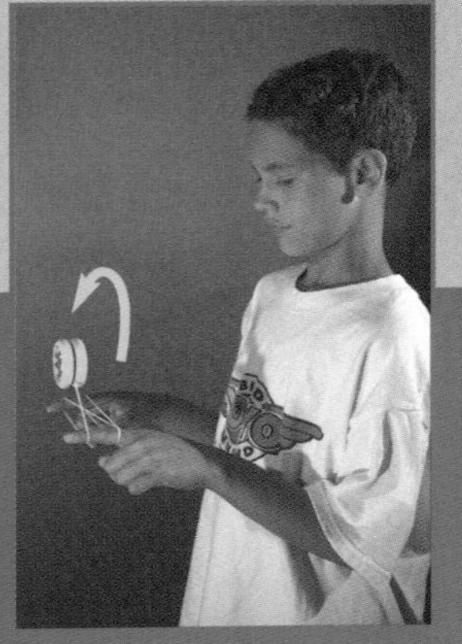

3. One more time around the free-hand index finger! Then catch that sucker!

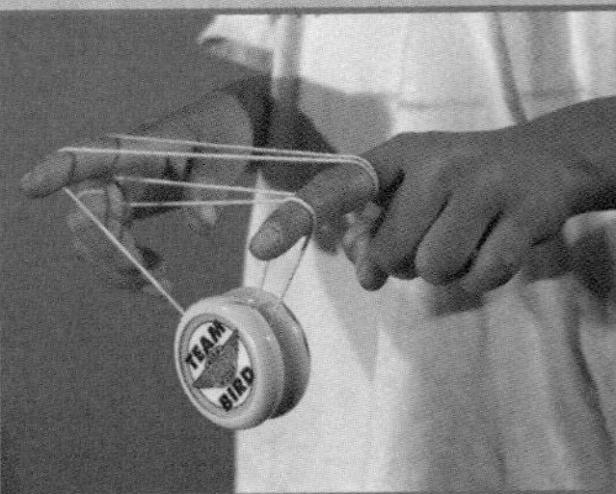

4. You did it! Didn't you? Now Dismount.

5. Here's what a successful Triple or Nothing looks like. Note that the yo-yo is on the outermost string. Remember to keep the first turns of string far down the fingers and away from the "catch" string. Now try *Quadruple* or Nothing.

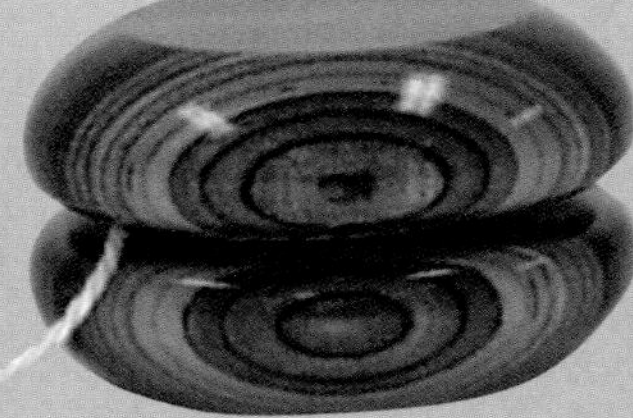

6. In the Triple or Nothing, you get a lot more Nothing if you mess up.

Reverse Double or Nothing

This is a cool trick. A quick change-up that spices up the normal Man on the Flying Trapeze. It can also be added into a flurry of sideways tricks.

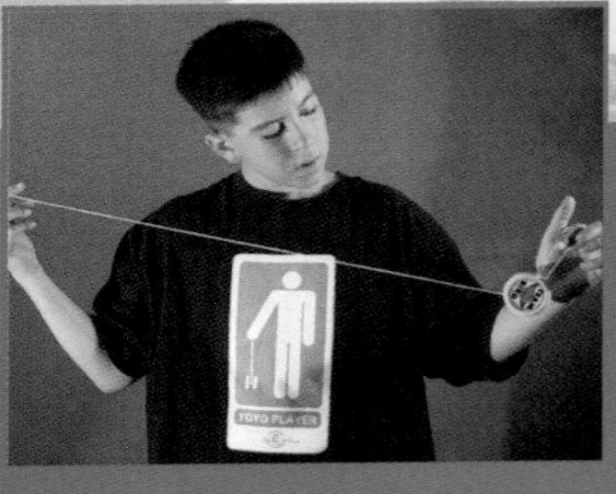

1. Start the Reverse Double or Nothing from a Man on the Flying Trapeze. Do a quick flip out to get the yo-yo off and swinging. Note the positions of the fingers of the free hand because ...

2. ... the string should be between the index and middle fingers of your free hand. Don't pinch them too tightly. You want the string to be able to slide. Now check this out ...

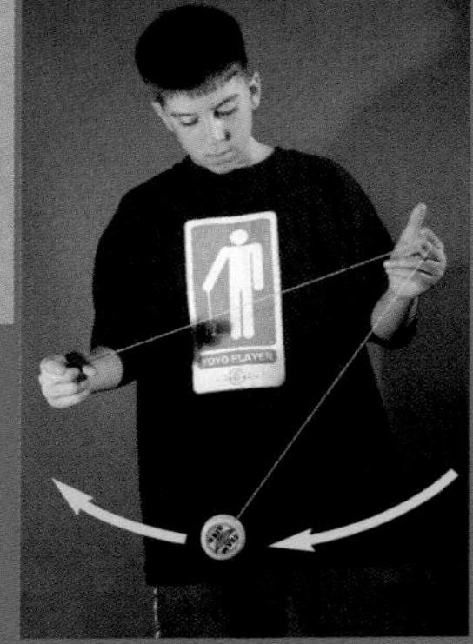

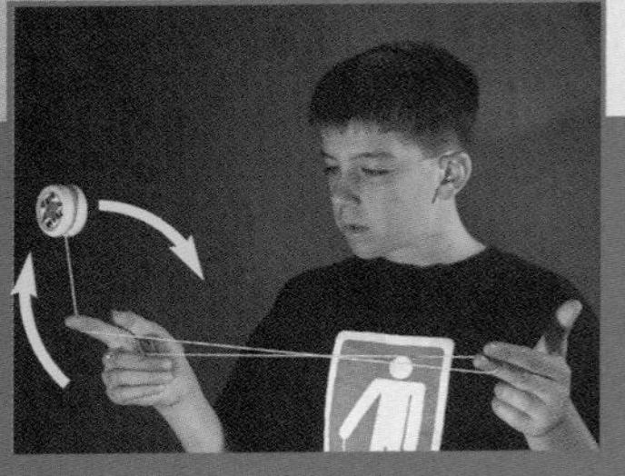

3. Let the yo-yo swing underneath both hands. Stick out your yo-yo-hand index finger so the yo-yo loops over it. And ...

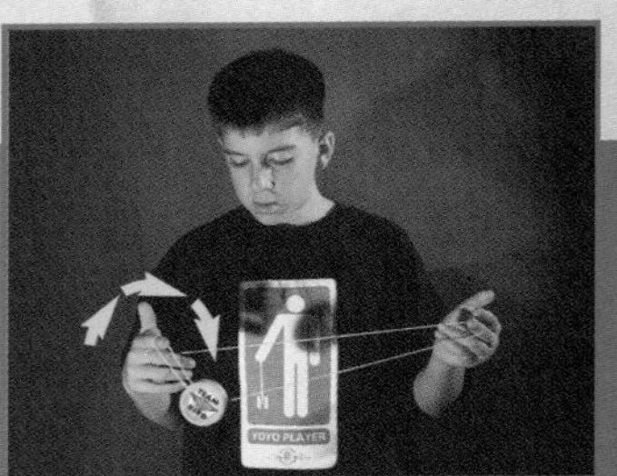

4. Catch it! This is how it should look when you've got the perfect Reverse Double or Nothing.

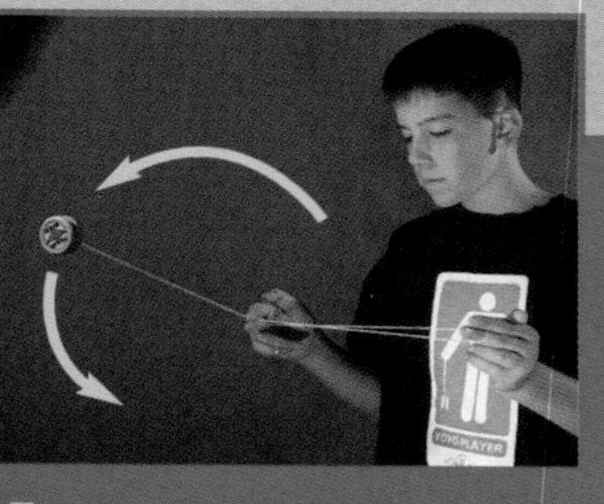

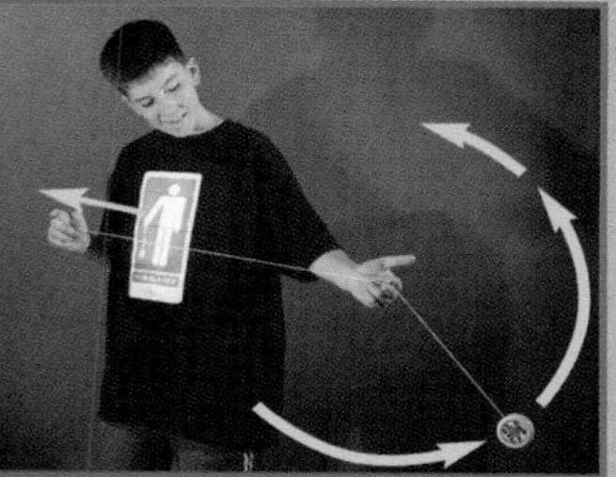

5. Pop the yo-yo off the string and let it swing back. Pull your hands a bit farther apart so you can catch the yo-yo ...

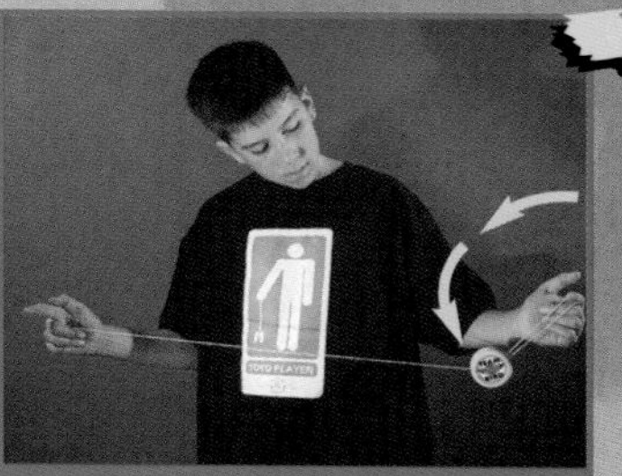

6. ... in a Man on the Flying Trapeze again! Pretty cool, huh?

TIP Warning! The spin of the yo-yo is reversed when it lands on the string. This can cause the yo-yo to "bite" the string and consequently run up the string and smack your finger. Ouch!

So, do *not* let the yo-yo stay there for long.

Ferris Wheel Dismount

The circus was never this fun. Let's say you find yourself at the end of a great run of tricks and you're in Man on the Flying Trapeze. How do you pull off a showy, high-flying dismount that has style and grace? Look no further, the Ferris Wheel is what you need.

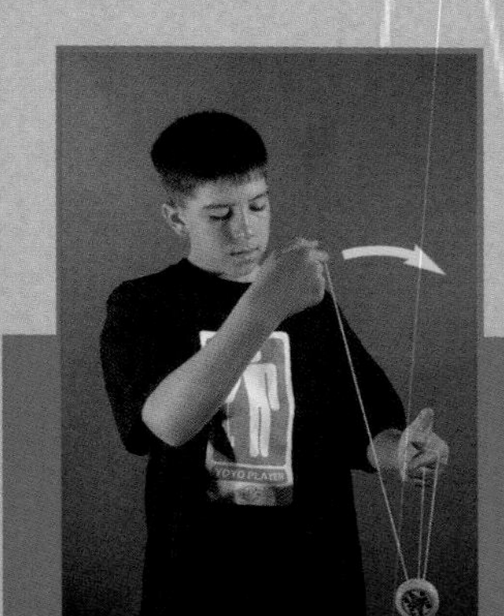

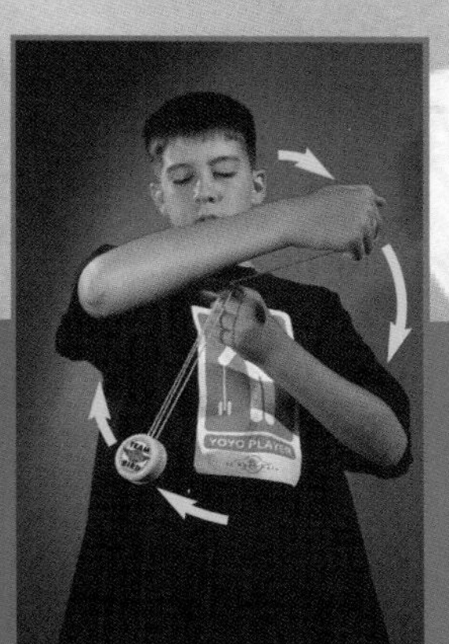

1. Bring your yo-yo hand over and drape the string over your freed hand's index finger. Don't pull on the string yet.

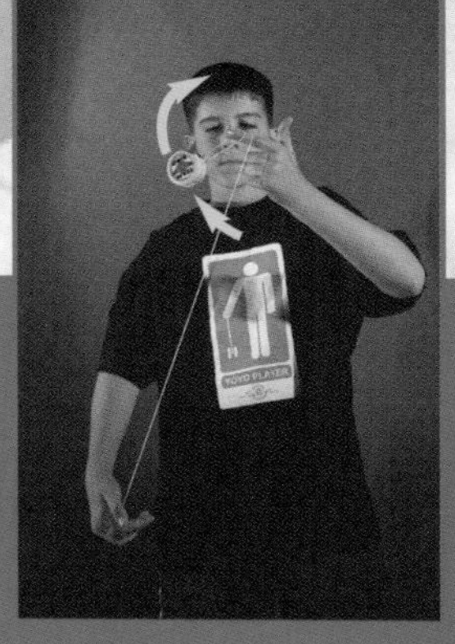

2. Swing the yo-yo over your free hand while pulling down with your yo-yo hand. Don't pull too hard! Try to keep your yo-yo hand as directly under your free hand as possible.

TIP Remember to keep that yo-yo hand directly under the free hand. If you don't, it will be hard to make your yo-yo fly straight up.

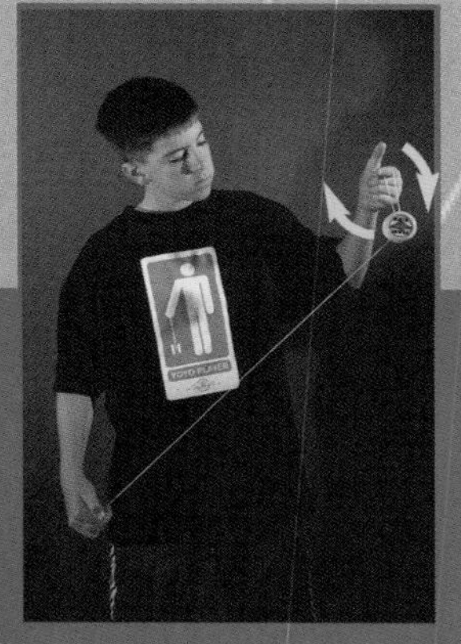

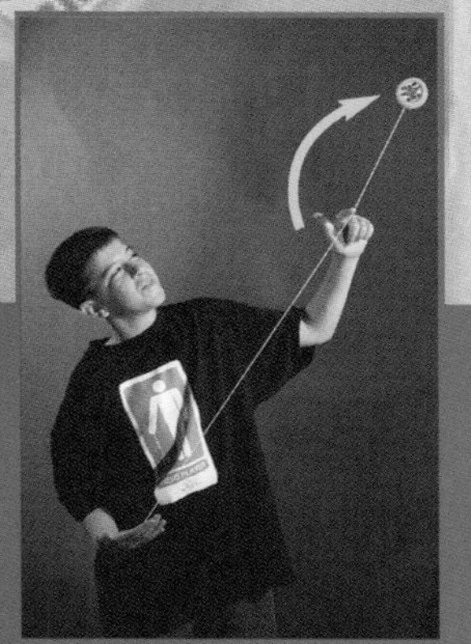

3. Keep the yo-yo swinging while pulling down with your yo-yo hand. The yo-yo should swing continuously so it circles like a Ferris Wheel. It should launch off the string straight up. Tug and it will land ...

4. ... back in your hand. Ride the Ferris Wheel again and again.

Trivi-Yo

CHICO 1969 NORTHERN CALIFORNIA REGIONAL YoYo CONTEST

The yo-yo is not just a toy. Physicists around the world use yo-yos to demonstrate the laws of thermodynamics. They also use them in experiments for the classes they teach.

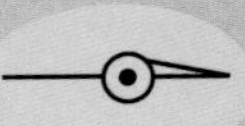

Lindy Loops

This is a little trick without much flash. Lindy Loops, however, are difficult and add a nice counterpoint to the huge, looping moves that you see so often. So don't forget them while yo-yoing.

TIP Attention! The string is now looped around the axle *twice*. Some yo-yos will bite when you do this and bind up on the string.

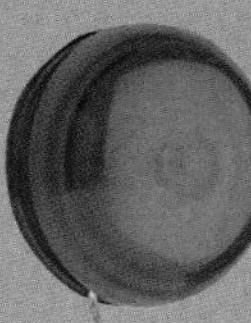

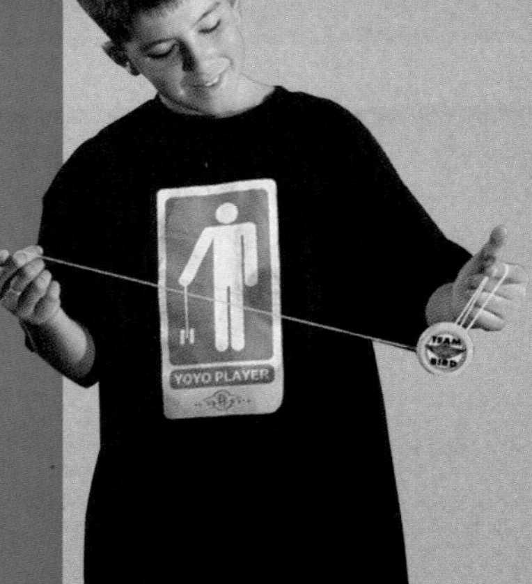

1. Start with a Man on the Flying Trapeze. Make sure there's a bit of slack in the string because you're going to take that yo-yo and …

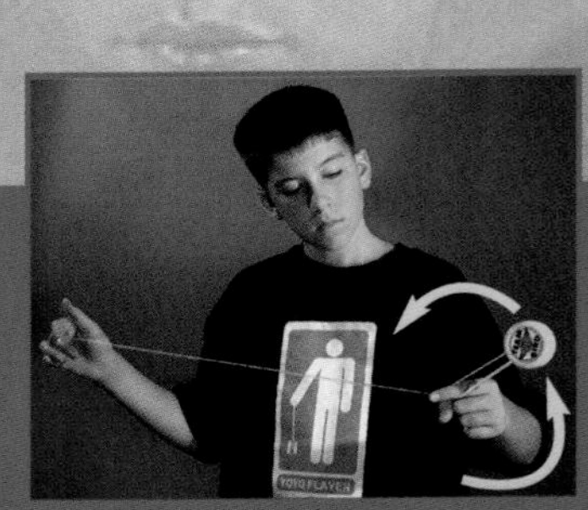

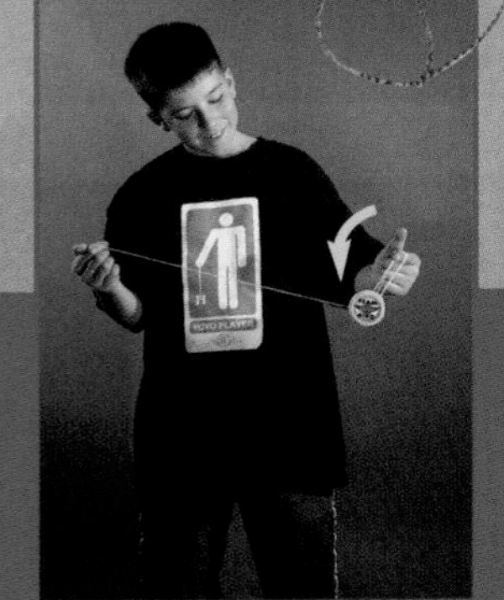

2. … loop it over your free-hand index finger. Catch it on the string and you've done it. Simple, right?

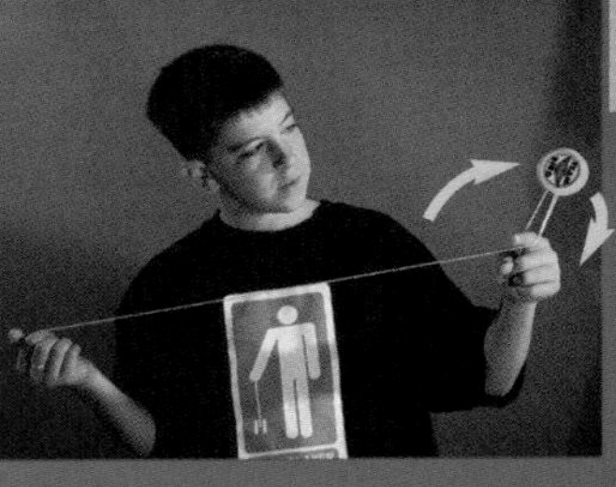

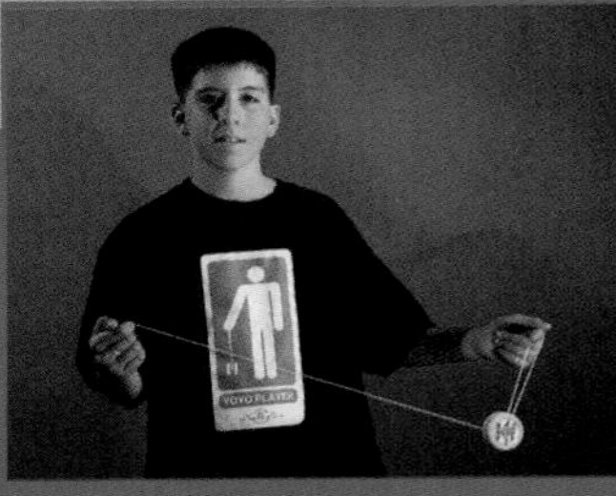

3. To get out of the Lindy Loop, simply hop the yo-yo back over your finger and into Man on the Flying Trapeze. Can you do more Lindy Loops?

TIP You can do Lindy Loops in other tricks as well. Try to do one into a finished Double or Nothing. Or in an Under Mount and then an Over Under Mount. How about in a backward double or nothing? How many tricks can you find where a Lindy Loop would work?

Barrel Rolls

Barrel Rolls are a sweet little maneuver. They show up in other tricks. Plus, they can be very satisfying to pull off correctly. More fun, you might say, than a Barrel of Mon … oh, never mind.

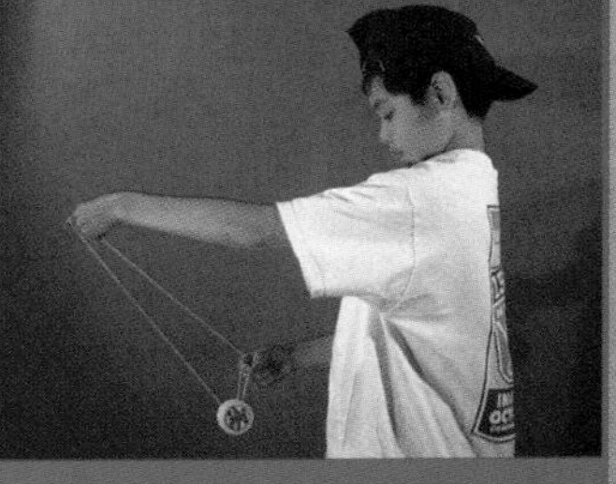

1. Begin with your standard Over-Under Mount. Nothing too fancy—yet.

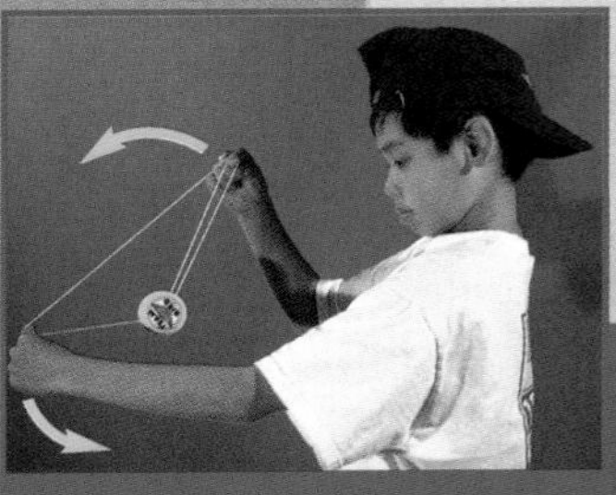

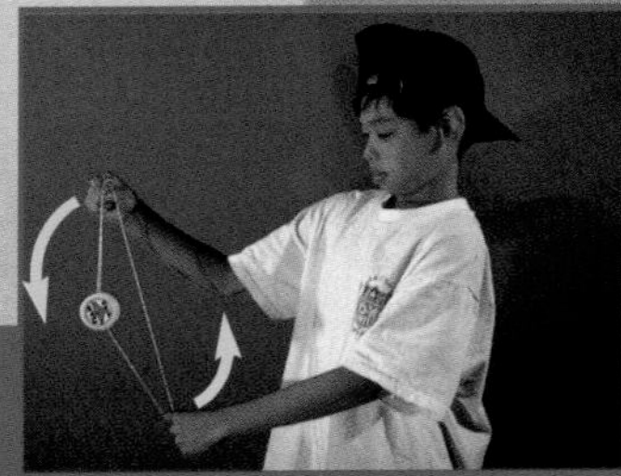

2. Now, in a continuous motion, move your hands in a circular pattern. The yo-yo, still sleeping of course, will come up with the string, then fall forward onto the front string.

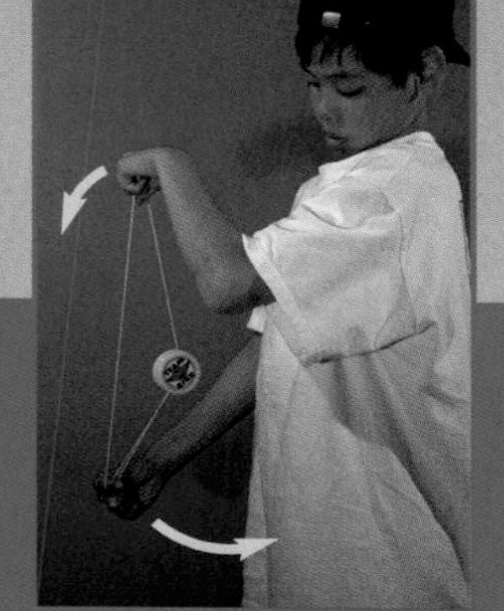

3. Keep going with your hands. Keep moving them in a circle.

4. The yo-yo will swing forward again and then, abracadabra, you'll be back in the Over-Under Mount position. That's one Barrel Roll. There is, however, a small price to pay ...

Twisted String

5. Doing several Barrel Rolls in a row can twist the string around your yo-yo hand's index finger. What do you do?

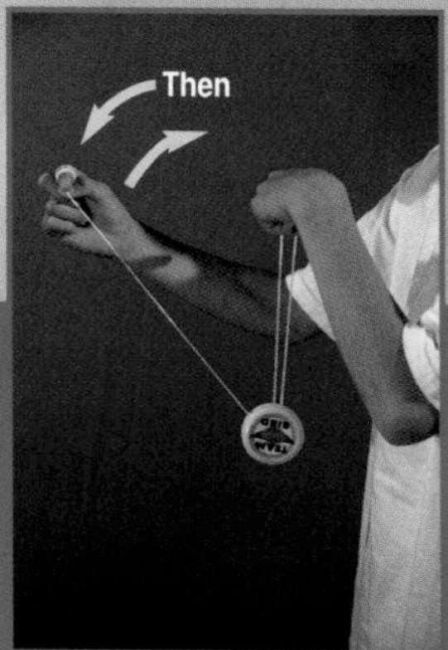

6. Unwind it! Let the yo-yo fall onto the forward string, then pull back with your finger to let the string twirl off. Then it's a simple Dismount to get the yo-yo out and back to your hand.

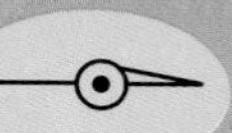

Barrel Rolls: Man on the Flying Trapeze

Barrel Rolls can also be done from Man on the Flying Trapeze. They are a little different when done this way, so watch carefully.

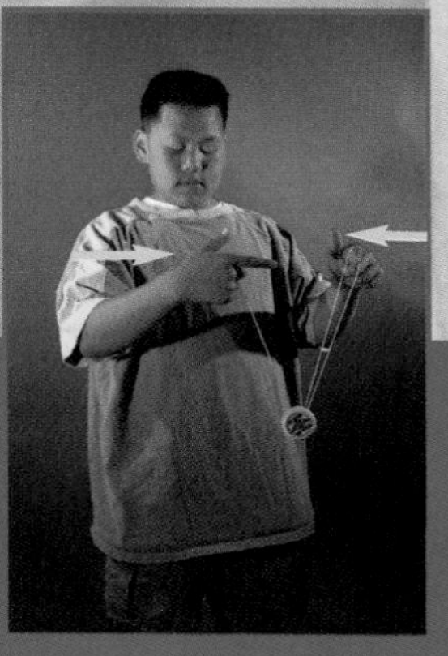

1. Start with the Man on the Flying Trapeze. Bring your hands together to let the yo-yo hang low.

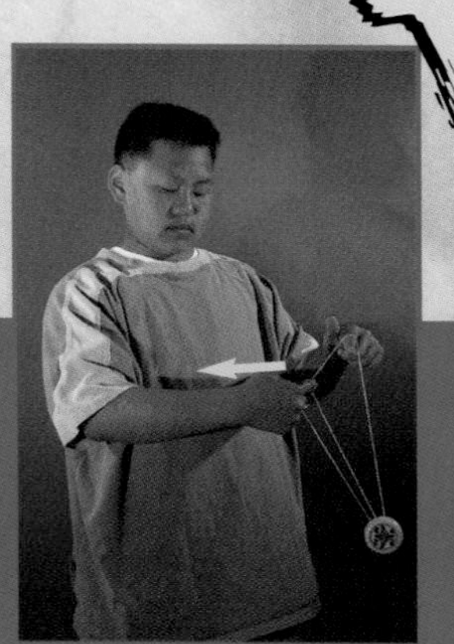

2. Pluck the string close to you and pull back on it.

TIP Notice that in this variation your Barrel Rolls are going in the opposite direction.

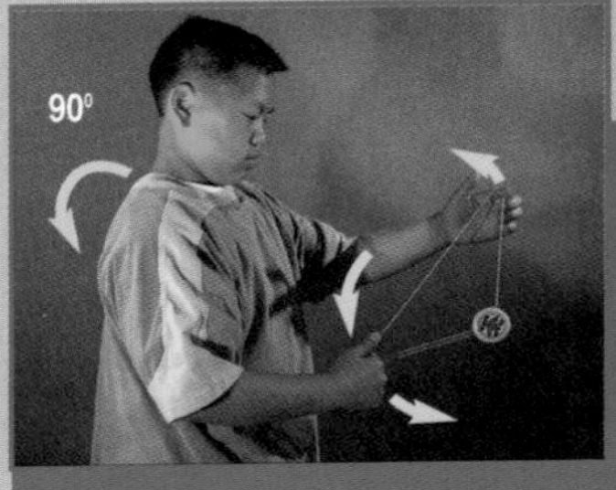

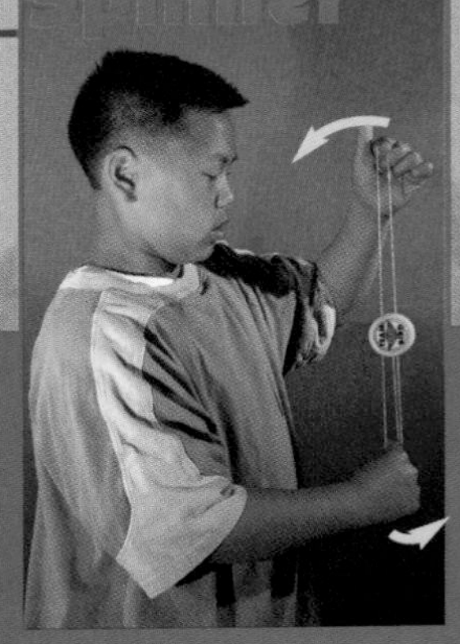

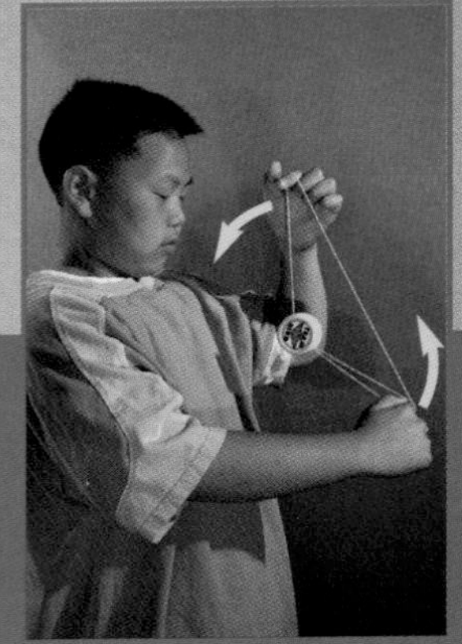

3. In one *fluid* motion, pull back on the string as you circle your hand under the yo-yo. This will cause the yo-yo to come up and then swing over to the back string.

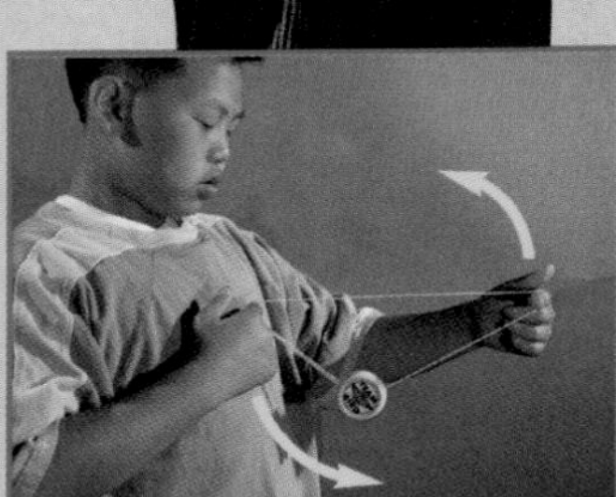

4. Keep that motion going and swing the yo-yo around again. It will swing up, then swing over to the back string.

5. Bingo! That's one Barrel Roll from Man on the Flying Trapeze. The Dismount is just the same as for the regular Barrel Roll.

Undercuts

Here's a trick that, like so many before it, looks easy when done well. But if your friends try to copy you just by watching, they may have a bad time. Undercuts will be important later on for a trick called Atom Bomb.

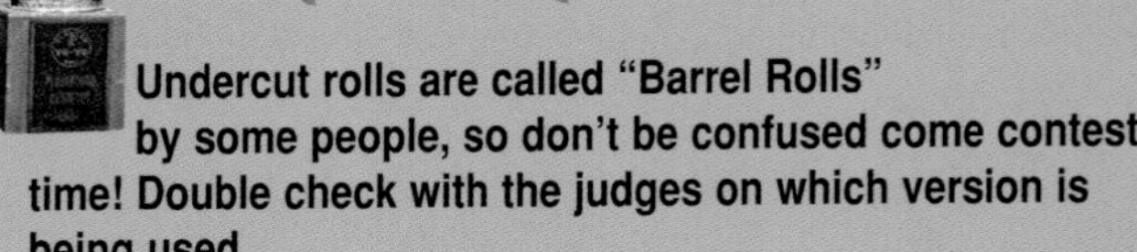

Competition Tip

Undercut rolls are called "Barrel Rolls" by some people, so don't be confused come contest time! Double check with the judges on which version is being used.

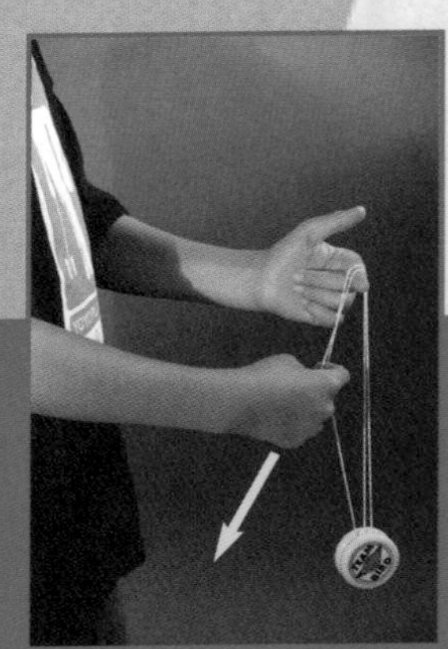

1. Start with a trusty Under Mount. Reach in with the index finger of your yo-yo hand and hook the string closest to your body.

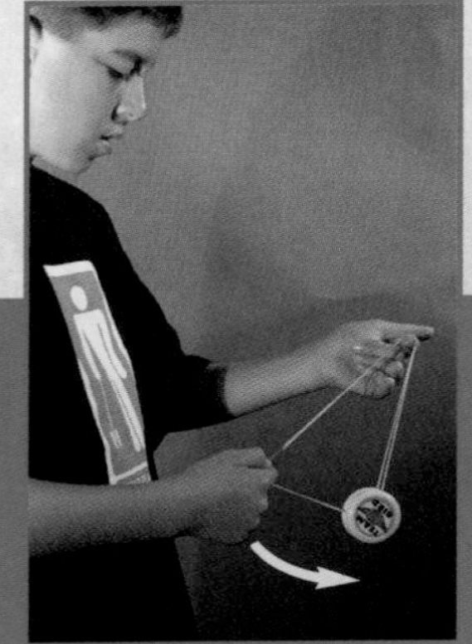

2. Pull the string down and around underneath the yo-yo. The yo-yo should swing from the front string to the back string.

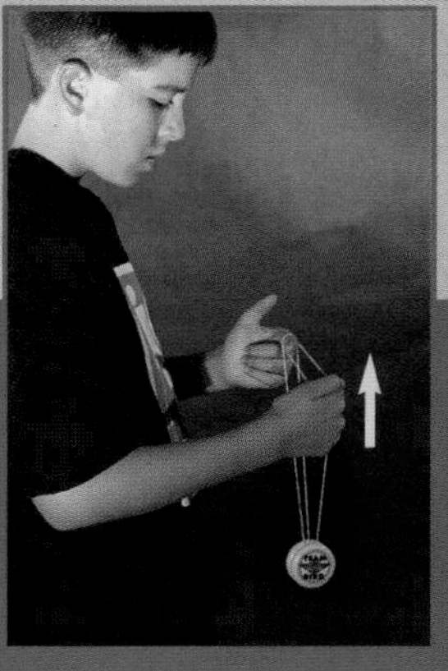

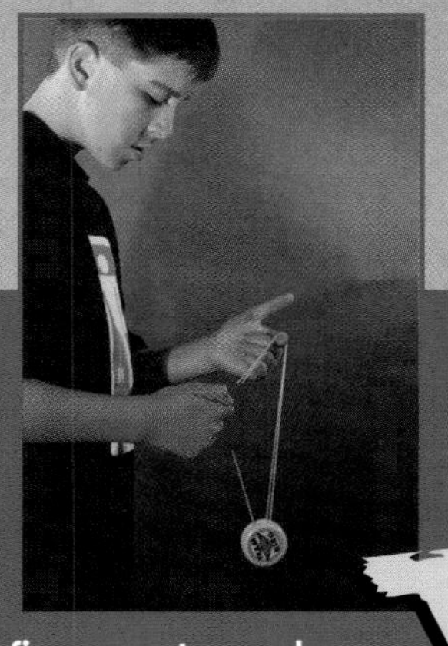

3. Bring your yo-yo-hand index finger up toward your free hand. The yo-yo will hang back in the starting position. There you go! One Undercut. Do more of them if you feel the need.

TIP Here's the trick. Make sure that after you do the Under Mount you bring your yo-yo hand *over* your free hand, just as you would for a Double Skin the Cat beginning. Don't let the string fall off your free-hand index finger or you won't be able to do the Undercut.

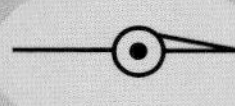

Somersault

Like the Undercuts, the Somersault is a deceptively difficult trick. You've already seen it as part of the Ferris Wheel Dismount, but it's a trick in and of itself. Let's tumble.

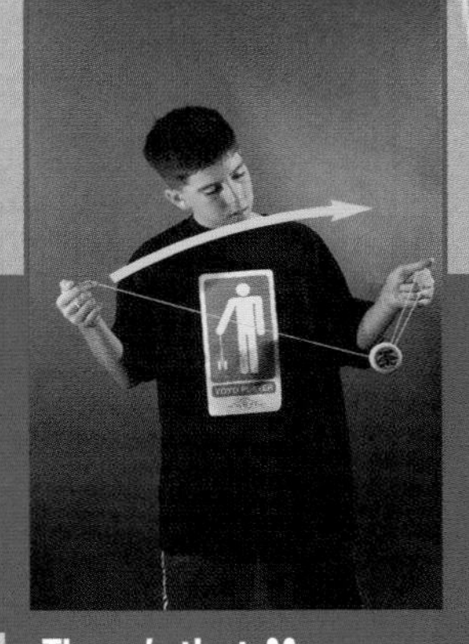

1. There's that Man on the Flying Trapeze again. He gets around. Now, bring your yo-yo hand near and a bit above your free hand.

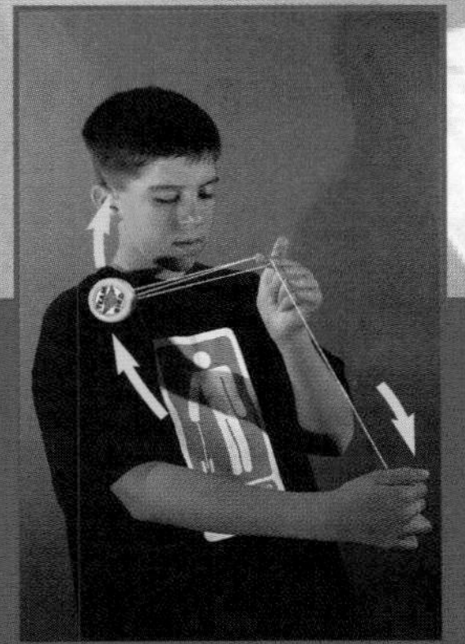

2. Start the yo-yo swinging away from your body as you pull down and around with your yo-yo hand. Keep that free hand still. Let the yo-yo orbit around your free-hand index finger.

3. When the yo-yo has looped back to the starting position, you're done! One Somersault.

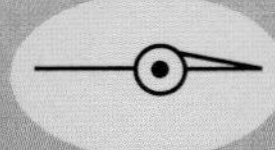

Backflip

The Backflip is an excellent companion to the Somersault because it's the exact opposite.

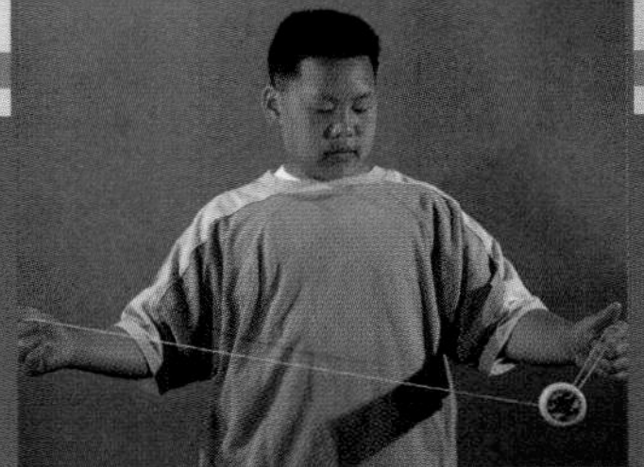

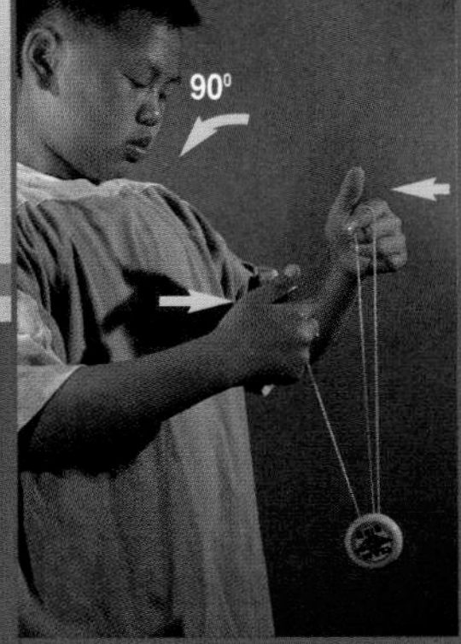

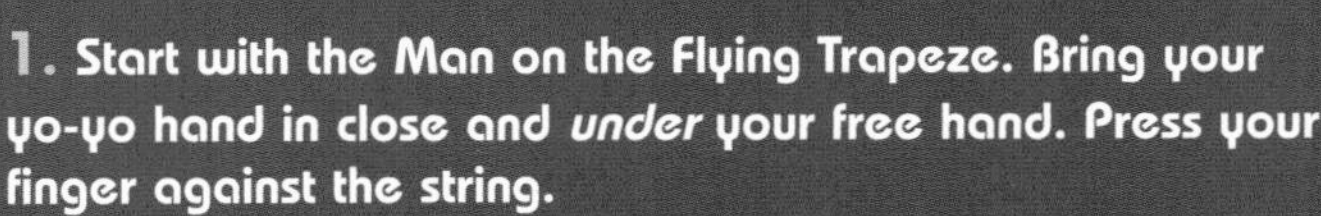

1. Start with the Man on the Flying Trapeze. Bring your yo-yo hand in close and *under* your free hand. Press your finger against the string.

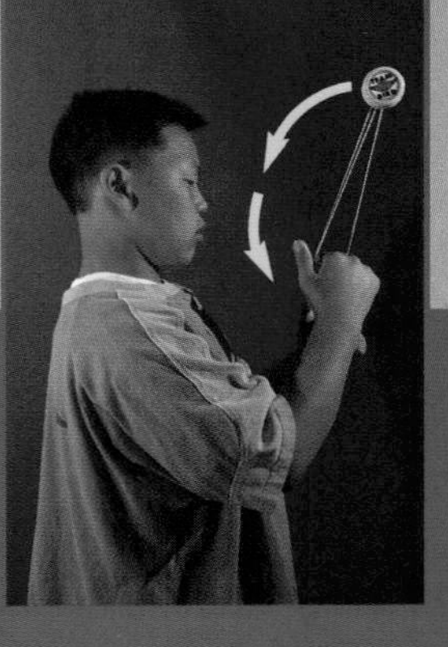

2. Swing the yo-yo away from your body and keep it going with your yo-yo hand on the string.

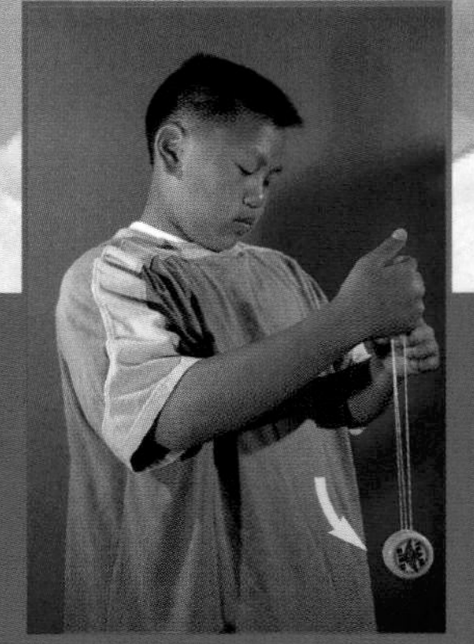
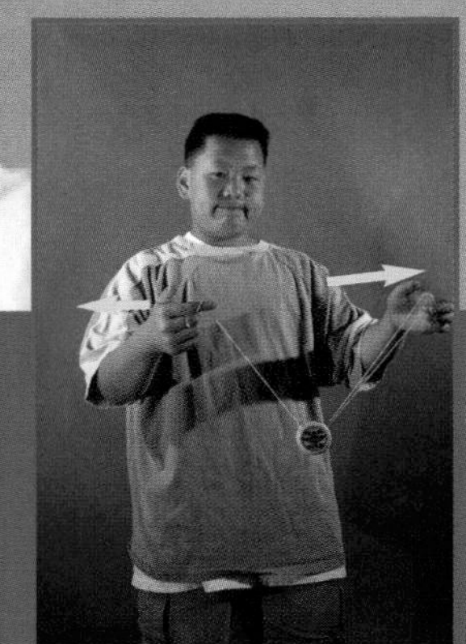

3. And here you are, back at the beginning again. That's a Backflip.

Try to jump back and forth from Somersault to Backflip to Somersault to Backflip. It looks cool!

Moving On

This is a massive section of Building Blocks. However, the moves and maneuvers you just learned in this section are more like puzzle pieces. Each one can be done before, after, or (sometimes) in the middle of other moves to make a seamless, fluid run of tricks.

That's where you want to be. You need to be able to link these pieces together if you want to be a real Spinner. We have given and will continue to give suggestions and personal favorites for trick runs, but in the end it's up to you.

Yo-yoing can be very satisfying when you can start putting these tricks together without a pause. Some of the tricks in the next section are just that—a continuous chain of advanced Building Blocks.

So we've coached you this far, and we're not going to give up on you now! Change the string, lube the axle, tape up your finger, and get ready for advanced tricks!

The Big Time

You made it! We know that some of you picked up this book and didn't know a Gravity Pull from a pushpin. And now look at you. Bravo!

There are lots of combinations for these advanced tricks. Some are built out of the Building Blocks you learned previously. There are also a few surprises and a couple of cool stand-alone tricks. Read on and keep spinning. There's nowhere to go but up—and down. And up again.

Tricks

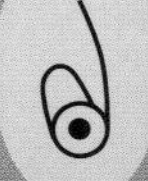

Atom Bomb

Right out of Building Blocks and into the atomic fire. This trick is a standard that combines a few of the Building Blocks you just learned.

1. You begin this one with the Under Mount. Then reach in to pluck the string closest to your body for an Undercut.

2. Do one Undercut (for now) and keep your finger between the strings. There should be two strings between the index finger of your yo-yo hand and your body.

TIP You can add in a lot of Undercuts and as many Somersaults as you want. At least until the string wraps up too much on your finger. Try for three of each!

3. Now pull your yo-yo hand back and then around your free hand. This will swing the yo-yo around in a Somersault.

4. The Somersault will also wrap string around your yo-yo hand's index finger. Pull that hand back to let the string twist off the finger. You're back in the Under Mount position. This, as you know, is the same as a completed Basic Front Mount. So pull your yo-yo hand back while swinging the yo-yo out in a Roll Away Dismount. (Review the intermediate Building Blocks if you need a refresher.) Bang! That's the Atom Bomb!

Remember to Loop out of the Atom Bomb!

Split the Atom: Basic

To continue with our physics lesson, we'll move on to Split the Atom. It's another series of connected Building Blocks formed into one impressive trick. Read the name carefully, though. This is just the Basic!

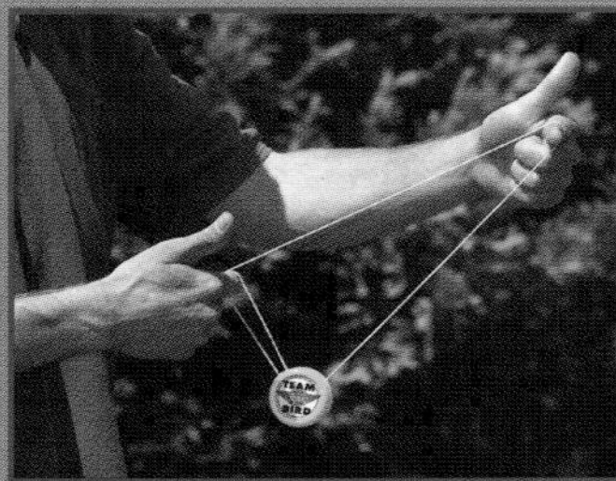

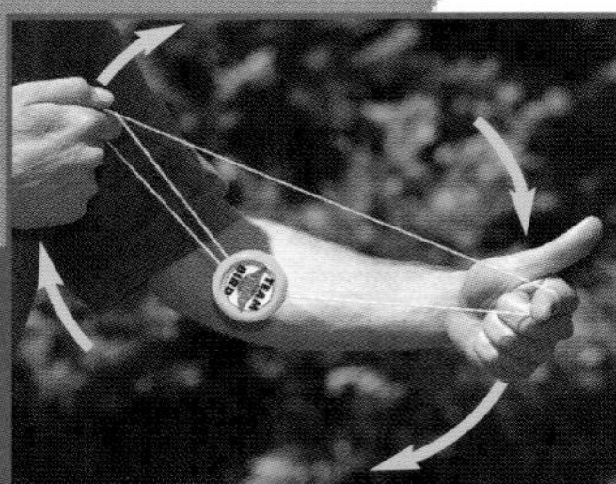

1. Start with an Over-Under Mount—also called a *Split* Mount (*Split* the Atom. Get it?). Circle your hands away from your body so the yo-yo swings onto the forward string. Like a piece of a Barrel Roll.

2. Keep your yo-yo hand still and bring your free hand forward to the front string. Circle that free hand up and start to move your yo-yo hand back and ...

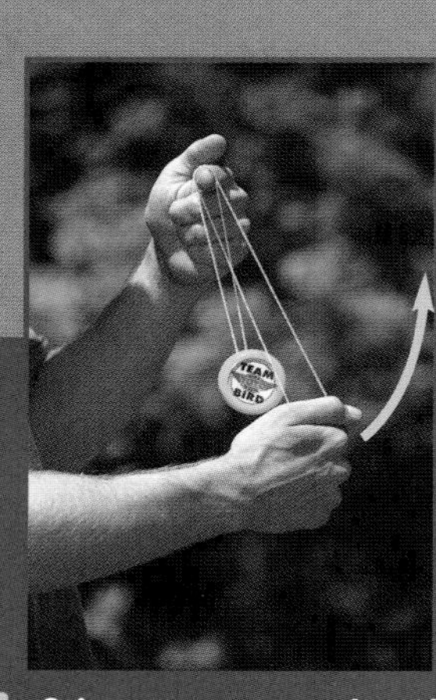

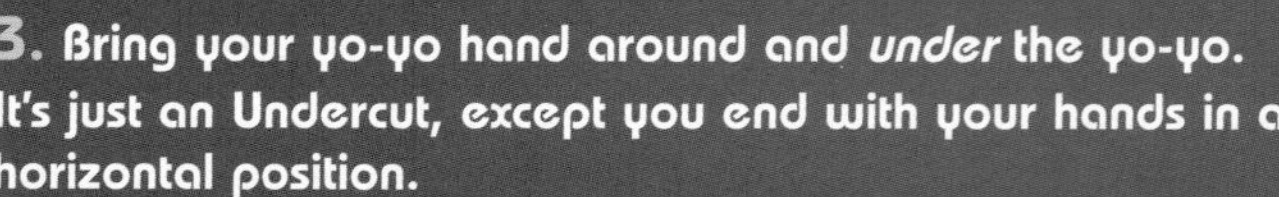

3. Bring your yo-yo hand around and *under* the yo-yo. It's just an Undercut, except you end with your hands in a horizontal position.

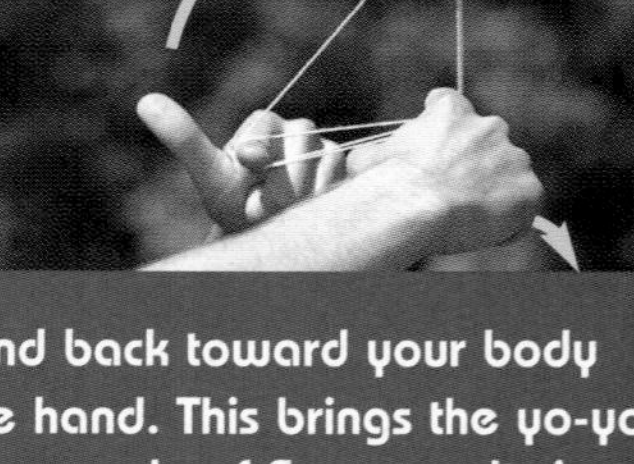

4. Now bring that yo-yo hand back toward your body and circle it around your free hand. This brings the yo-yo around in a Somersault. Do a couple of Somersaults just for kicks.

5. Just as in the Atom Bomb, these Somersaults will wrap string around the index finger of your yo-yo hand. So ...

6. Bring that yo-yo hand back to pull the string off your finger, and presto, you're in that familiar Basic Front Mount position. Do a Roll Away Dismount and a Loop to end Split the Atom.

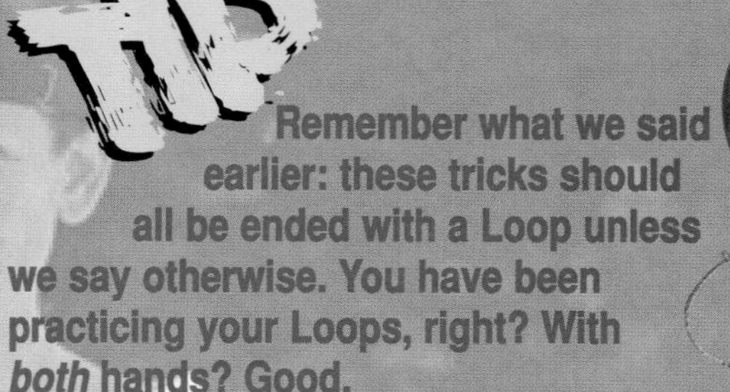

TIP Remember what we said earlier: these tricks should all be ended with a Loop unless we say otherwise. You have been practicing your Loops, right? With *both* hands? Good.

Split the Atom: Advanced

The Advanced Split the Atom is not as intimidating as it sounds. Well, maybe it is. If you know the Basic, then all you have to do is add a few elements. Spice it up, so to speak.

The following description assumes that you know the Basic Split the Atom, so if a part of the Advanced is not fully shown, you can find it in the description of the Basic.

1. This time, start with a Front Pinwheel that drops into an Over-Under Mount. This move is covered in the description of advanced Building Blocks in Chapter 7.

2. Do a quick Roll Over. It ends with the yo-yo still in the Under Mount, but puts a loop around your yo-hand index finger.

3. Circle your hands and let the yo-yo swing to the front string just as you did in the beginning of the Basic Split the Atom. This time, however, *keep circling* your hands so you're doing Barrel Rolls. Do a few of them and then ...

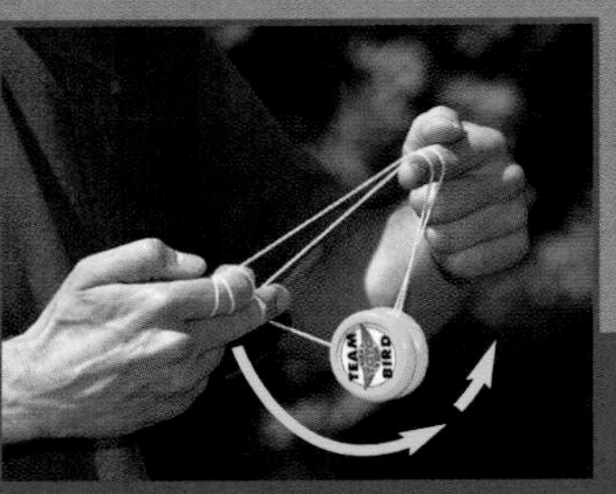
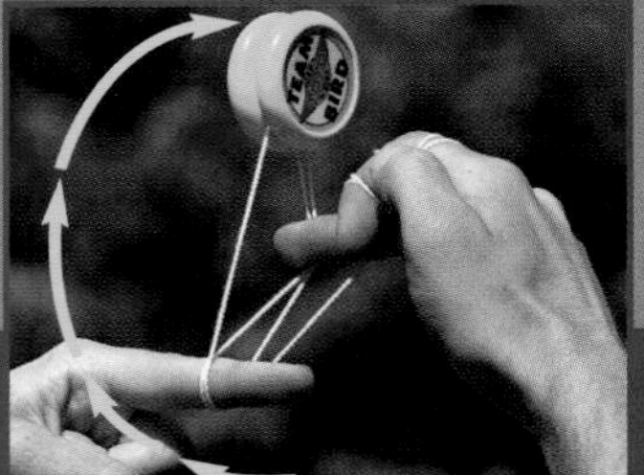
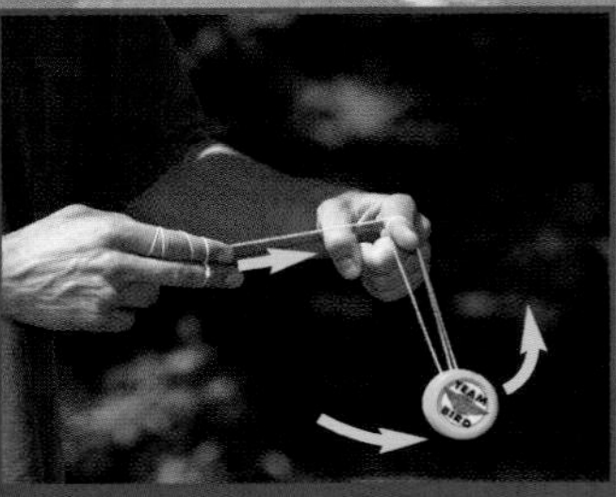

4. It's just the same as the Basic. Undercut with your yo-yo hand, do several Somersaults, then do a Roll Out Dismount. That wasn't so hard, was it?

5. Oh yeah, remember to Loop out of the Dismount.

Do the Undercut with the middle finger of your yo-hand.

Competition Tip

If the Advanced Split the Atom comes up in a competition, it will involve these elements:

- Three Front Pinwheels
- Three Barrel Rolls
- Three Somersaults
- Loop out of the Dismount

Hydrogen Bomb

If you ever get tired of Split the Atom, you can do it backward! The Hydrogen Bomb is a difficult trick, prone to tangling your string. Pull it off and you're going to break your arm patting yourself on the back. Then, at competition time, you'll find that it's a *standard* trick. Don't let that diminish your pride, though—you've earned it.

There are many variations; this is the one we use.

1. Earlier you came across the Hydrogen Bomb Mount. Guess what it's used for? That's right, this trick. Get into the Mount and the fun begins.

2. Circle your free hand under the yo-yo. Bring your yo-yo hand slightly back. Use the motion to swing the yo-yo onto the back string.

If you're having trouble keeping the yo-yo on the string during all the string tricks, you may have too much tension. Make sure your hands aren't so far apart that there's no slack in the string. If you're holding the string too taut, the yo-yo will bounce off.

3. Keep circling that free hand. Bring it up and against the two strings hanging from your yo-yo hand.

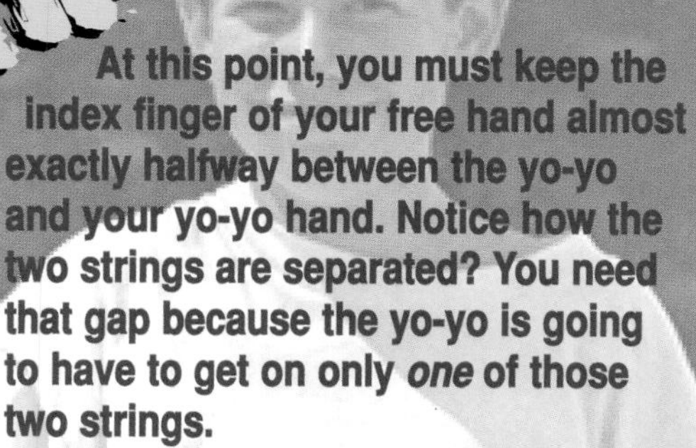

TIP

At this point, you must keep the index finger of your free hand almost exactly halfway between the yo-yo and your yo-yo hand. Notice how the two strings are separated? You need that gap because the yo-yo is going to have to get on only *one* of those two strings.

TIP

This is the string you need to hit.

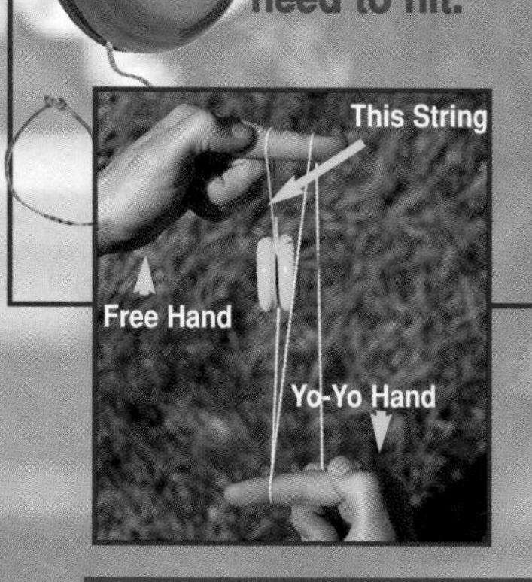

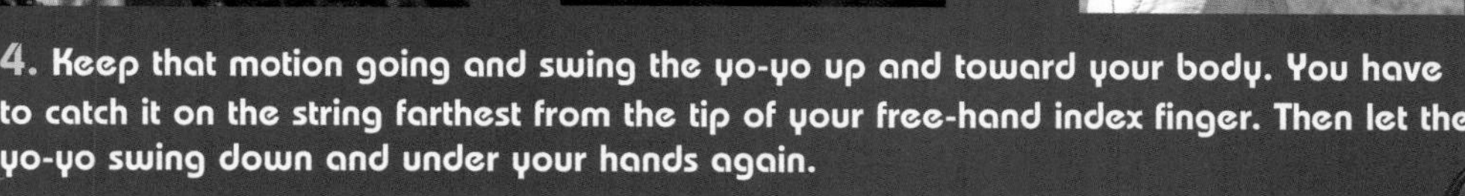

4. Keep that motion going and swing the yo-yo up and toward your body. You have to catch it on the string farthest from the tip of your free-hand index finger. Then let the yo-yo swing down and under your hands again.

5. Now let the string slide off the index finger of your yo-yo hand. Bring your yo-yo hand forward to get it in front of your free hand. Does this position look familiar?

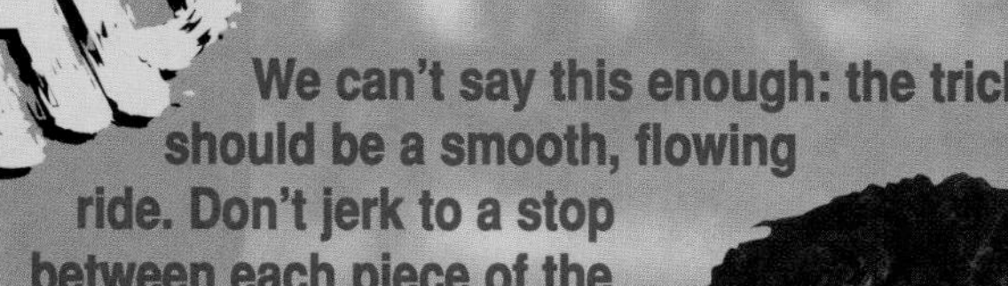

TIP

We can't say this enough: the trick should be a smooth, flowing ride. Don't jerk to a stop between each piece of the trick. Keep the motions going, making changes in direction as smooth as possible.

This tip is true for all the tricks like the Hydrogen Bomb.

Trivi-Yo

King George IV used a yo-yo! A painting of the monarch as a child shows him with one.

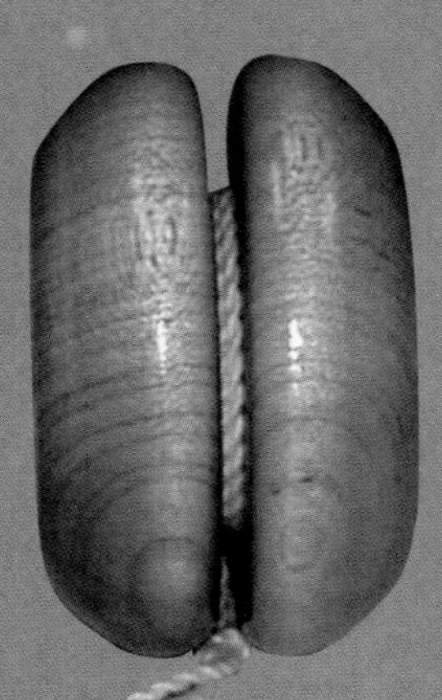

6. It's the position for the Ferris Wheel Dismount! Swing that yo-yo around and back into your hand. You've just built a Hydrogen Bomb.

Roller Coaster

This one is a nod to Dennis McBride, a Yo-Yo Master to whom we attribute this move.

Guess what? You know every part of this trick except one transition. Each part of the Roller Coaster has been covered earlier. This is a bare-bones description. Trust us, you know it already. We're just showing you how to put the pieces together.

1. Start with a World Tour.

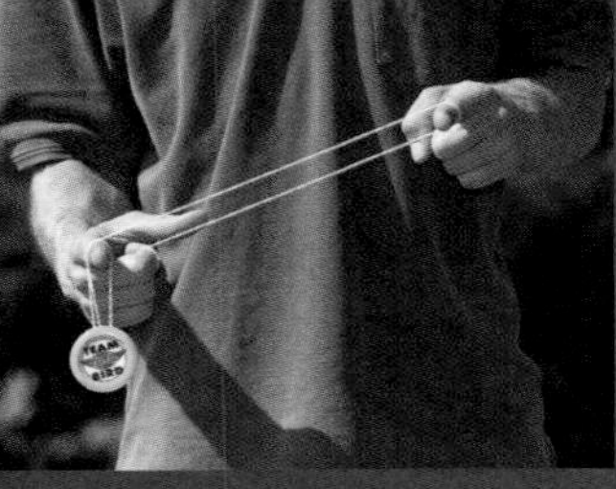

2. Stick out the index finger of your free hand and go into a Roller Coaster Mount. Remember to get your hands vertical.

3. Pop the yo-yo out of the Roller Coaster Mount, back around your free hand, and into the Reverse Double or Nothing. Tricky, isn't it?

TIP This is a *hard* trick. Practice the various pieces of the trick (especially the transition from Double to Triple or Nothing) by themselves. Once you have them down pat, practice linking them together.

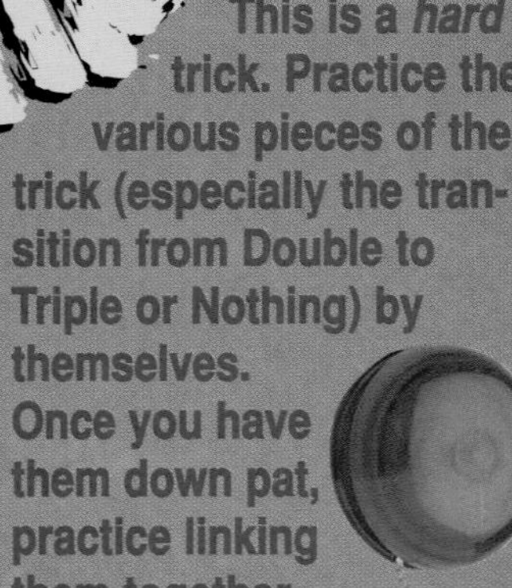

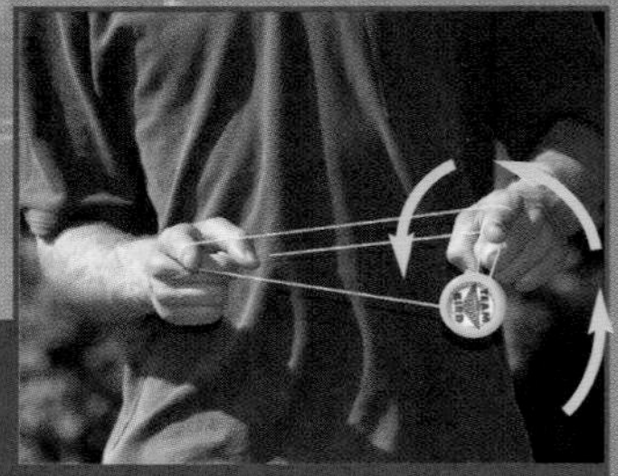

4. Flick the yo-yo out of the Reverse, back around your free hand, continuing around the yo-yo hand, and then into a Double or Nothing! Remember to give the yo-yo the string it needs to get around.

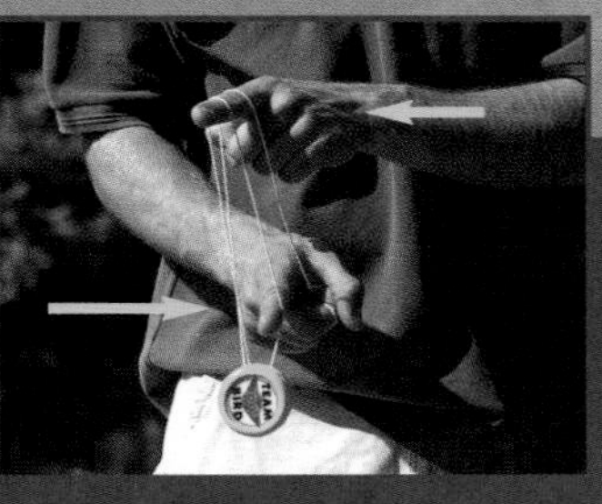

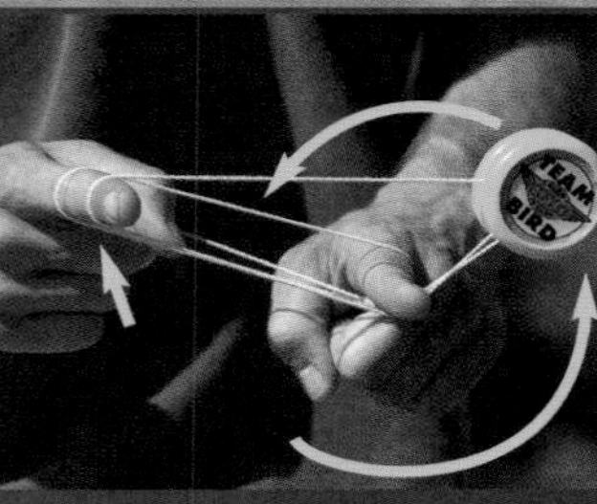

5. Here's the part you don't know yet: the transition from Double or Nothing into Triple or Nothing. Bring your hands close together. Put the index finger of your yo-yo hand into the loop of string on your free-hand index finger. Then pull your hands slightly apart. Swing the yo-yo over your free hand …

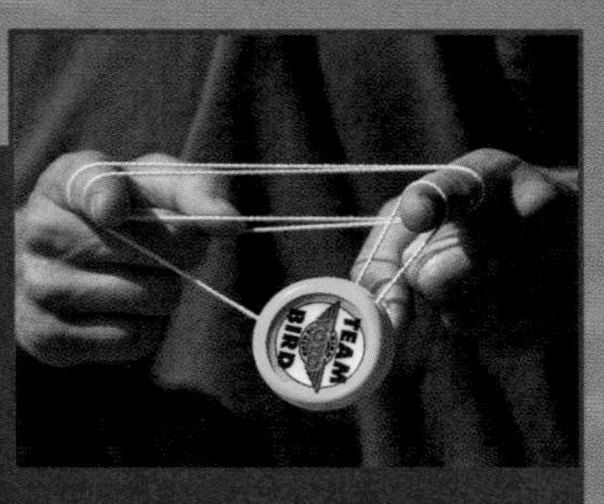

6. … and catch it on the *outermost* string. Presto, you're in Triple or Nothing! Do a flip out of the Triple or Nothing and the yo-yo lands neatly in your hand. Right?

Reach for the Moon

Of all the tricks in this book, Reach for the Moon is arguably the most elegant. The movements are simple and quiet, and the yo-yo seems to go slowly. It's even got a good name. And, to the person who doesn't know, Reach for the Moon seems impossible.

Here's how to do the impossible.

1. This is the basic stance for Reach for the Moon. Your arm will not move much at all. The action for this trick is in your wrist and hand.

2. The first throw should be up and in front of your arm. It should be very, very light. Just enough to get the yo-yo up there. You should *not* tug the string to get the yo-yo back down. Not only will you mess up the trick, but you might tug the yo-yo into your nose.

3. As the yo-yo comes back, turn your wrist in a small U motion. Mostly, you just let the yo-yo's momentum carry it around. Giving your wrist a small flick at the bottom of the U will send it back up into the second throw.

4. The second shot will end up slightly to the inside of your arm. Again, do *not* yank the yo-yo back down.

5. As the yo-yo comes back, follow the steps described before. Let the momentum carry it most of the way and then give a small flick to send it back up. Reach for the Moon should seem almost effortless.

TIP A good exercise for Reach for the Moon is to make the first throw and just let it fall back down. The yo-yo should simply fall by your shoulder. This gets you used to keeping your arm still.

Magic

Here's a quick little string trick that requires a long Sleeper and some fancy finger work. Amaze your friends!

1. Throw a Sleeper that will last for a long time. Then drape the string over the top of your free hand. Keep your fingers spread.

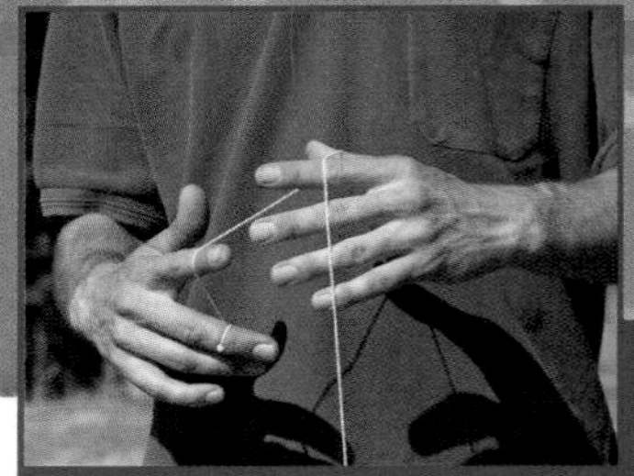

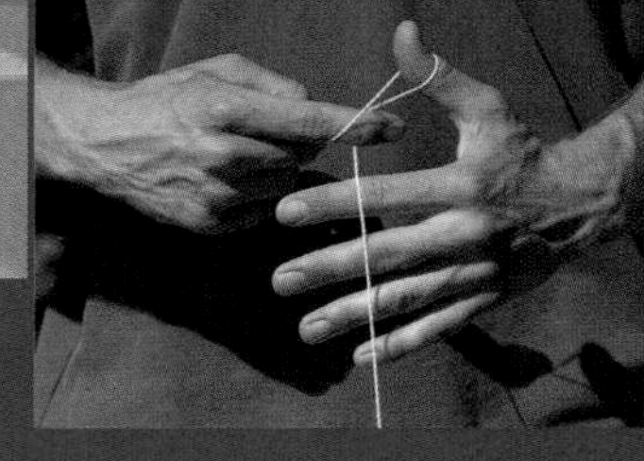

2. Reach the index finger of your yo-yo hand *under* the string. Then place it *on top* of the string between the thumb and index finger of your free hand. Pull down to get a good amount of slack.

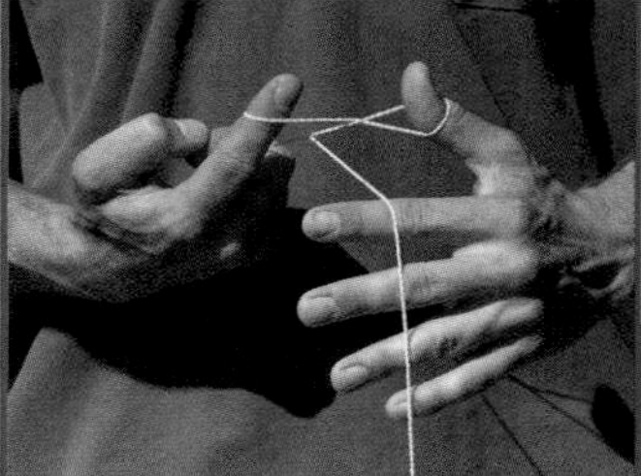

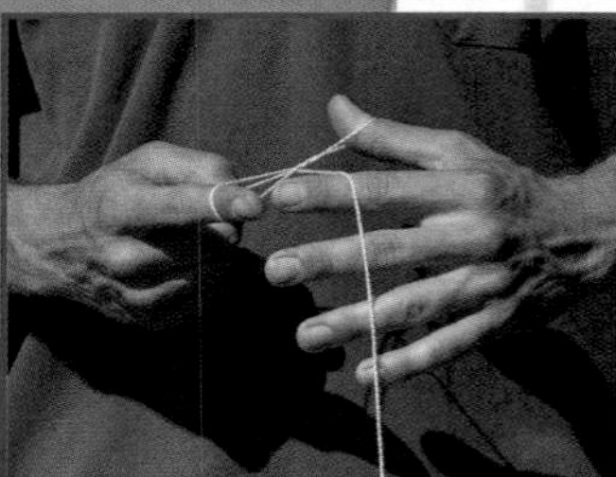

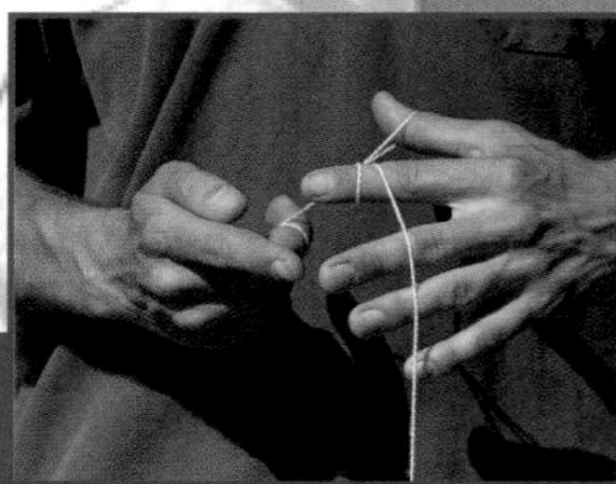

3. Pull the loop around the index finger of your yo-yo hand back *under* the string. Turn your finger clockwise (counterclockwise for lefties) so the loop has a twist in it. Take that loop and put it over the index finger of your free hand.

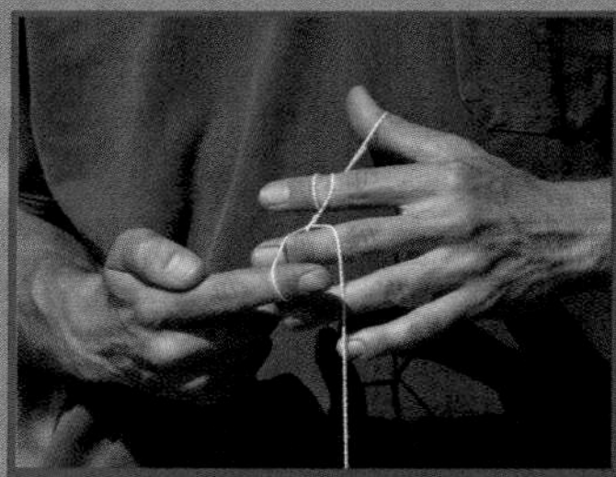

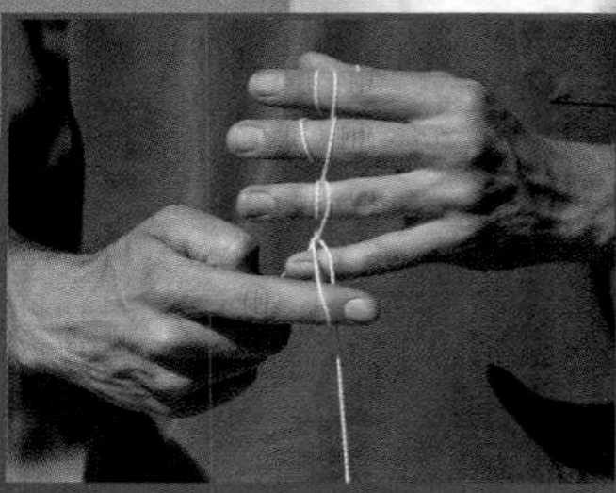

4. Now repeat that exact process on all the fingers of your free hand. Go under the string, pull down, twist the loop, place it on the finger.

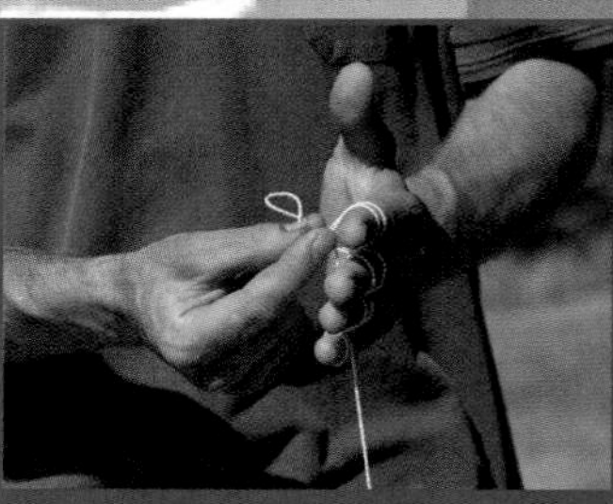

5. Wave your magic wand and slyly slip the loop off the thumb of your free hand.

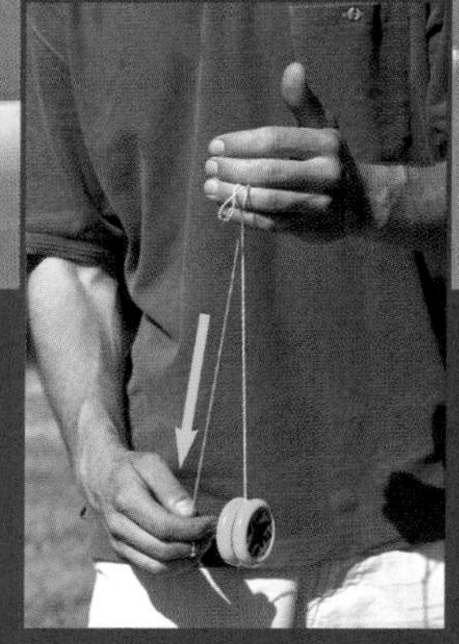

6. Then pull back with your yo-yo hand and watch the loops magically slide off your fingers without a hitch. Now give a tug and return the yo-yo. Magic!

Drop in the Bucket

Here's a Thaddaeus Winzenz original! Not only has this trick shown up throughout the yo-yo world, the Drop in the Bucket is a string trick whose name actually makes sense. You'll see.

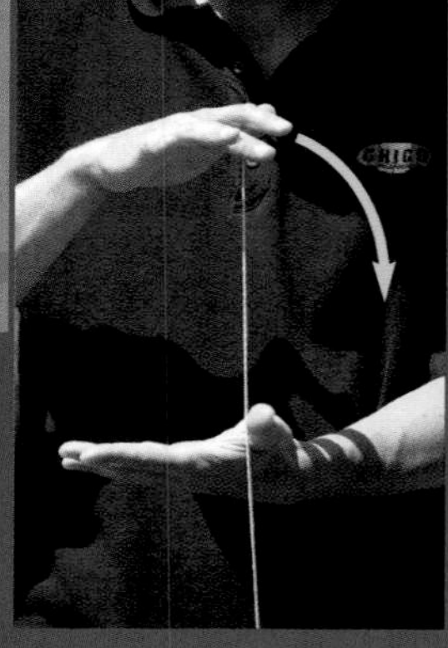

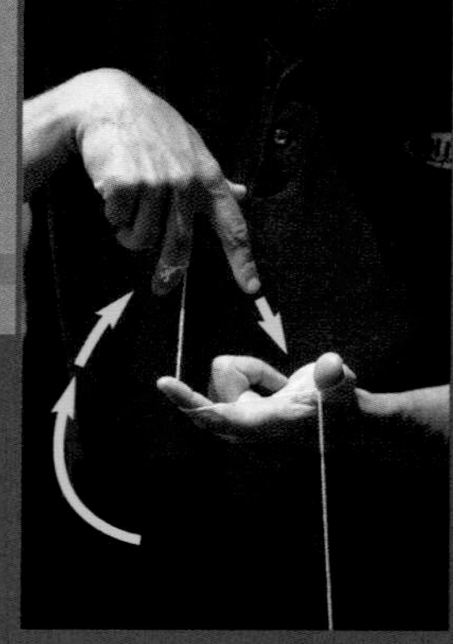

1. Get a good Break Away into a Sleeper going and hold out your free hand, palm up. Put your free-hand thumb and index finger on each side of the string. Wrap the string around the thumb, under your free hand, and then between your free-hand index and middle fingers.

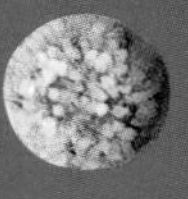

2. With the index finger of your yo-yo hand, pluck the string above the yo-yo and pull. Make sure it comes up *between* your free hand and the part of the string on your thumb and index finger.

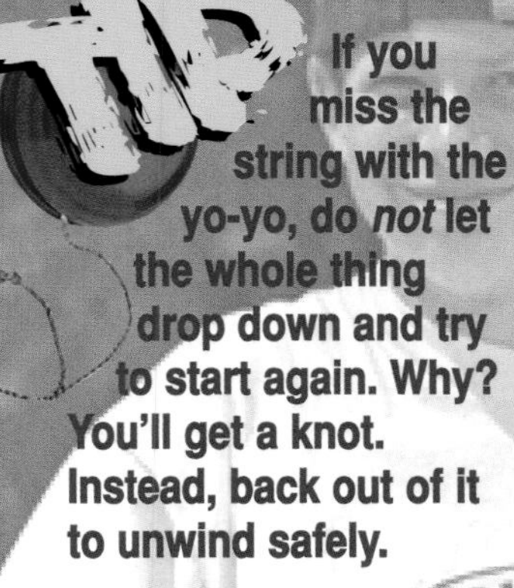

TIP If you miss the string with the yo-yo, do *not* let the whole thing drop down and try to start again. Why? You'll get a knot. Instead, back out of it to unwind safely.

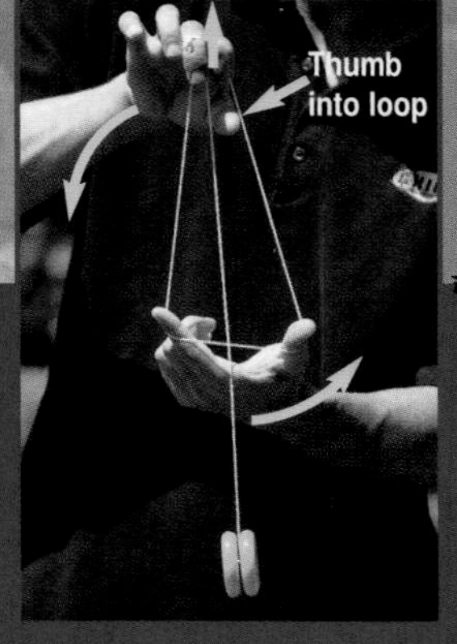

3. Place the string onto the thumb of your yo-yo hand. Make sure there is about this much string between your two hands.

TIP You can do this trick from Around the World. Or, for added style, bounce the yo-yo in and out of the bucket a few times before ending the trick.

4. In one fluid motion, swing the yo-yo up and catch it in the "bucket." Give it a little slack so it sags on the catch string. Then pull your hands apart and the yo-yo will pop back out.

Punching Bag

The Punching Bag provides a stark contrast to tricks like Reach for the Moon. Definite effort goes into this trick. That doesn't mean that you should get sloppy, though. It just means you should practice making this trick smooth.

Remember Hop the Fence? This is a Hop the Fence straight out in front of you.

1. Start with a Forward Pass. Do not turn your hand palm up. Keep your hand in the position it would be in for Hop the Fence.

2. Notice the hand position here. When the yo-yo comes back, guide it to loop *under* your hand and around. This will make it curve over the top of your hand before you send it out …

3. Into another Forward Pass. Repeat this continuously and you'll be doing the Punching Bag.

TIP At first, you may find that your hand keeps creeping farther up with each loop. Concentrate on keeping your hand in a set area. It will go up and down but shouldn't get higher and higher.

TIP You can also start the Punching Bag with a Hop the Fence. Start hopping and then gradually work the yo-yo up until it's going out at more than 45 degrees from your body.

Vertical Loops

If the Punching Bag was a Hop the Fence straight in front of you, a Vertical Loop is Hop the Fence straight up! The same rules and tips that applied to the Punching Bag also apply to Vertical Loops, so you may want to refer back to the Punching Bag.

1. Here's where you start. Don't wait too long or your arm will get tired.

2. Throw the yo-yo up. Simple enough, but what do you do when it comes back down?

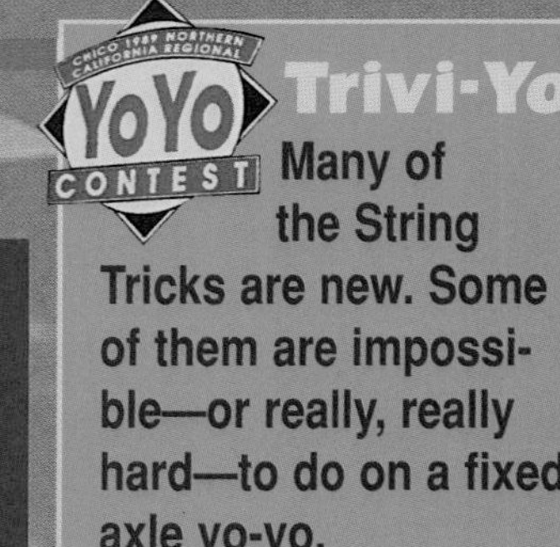

Trivi-Yo

Many of the String Tricks are new. Some of them are impossible—or really, really hard—to do on a fixed axle yo-yo.

Competition Tip

For competitions, the yo-yo has to stay between your shoulders and knees. No lower, no higher. Like the strike zone in baseball.

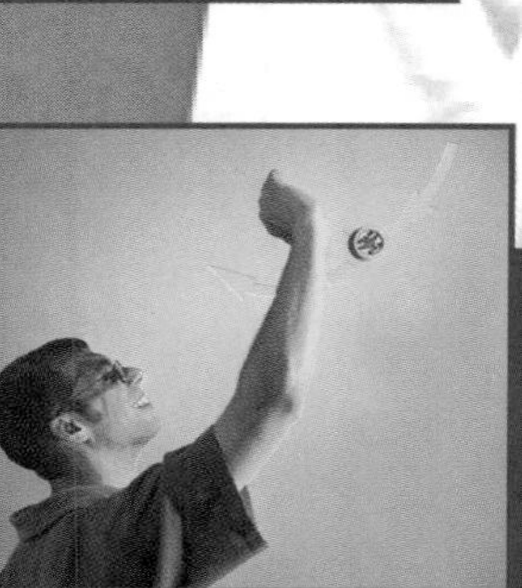

3. Guide the yo-yo in under your hand and then around and out over your hand. Vertical Loops are much more vertical than Reach for the Moon. They need a bit more power to launch.

4. Pop the yo-yo back up and then repeat the process. Remember the Punching Bag tip about keeping your hand in a set area.

Retro Around the World

This is simply Around the World backward. It tests the eyes in the back of your head. Practice this one outside, maybe with a helmet.

1. Toss the yo-yo like you would a sleeper. Send the yo-yo around in the direction opposite that of Around the World.

2. Let the yo-yo circle around and then call it back to your hand. There you go!

Regeneration of Spin

This almost doesn't belong among advanced tricks. It could be a section all by itself. But this is the point where you should be frustrated by having to catch your yo-yo and then throw it again to get to another trick. Wouldn't it be nice if you could keep the yo-yo spinning without catching it?

Well, there is a way to do this. No, it's not a motorized yo-yo. It's a technique called "Regeneration of Spin."

When your yo-yo starts to slow down, as it most certainly will if you've been doing a bunch of string tricks, you can use the Regeneration to get the speed up again. This will let you go on and perform more tricks without losing a beat.

How's it done? Let's start off simple, just to get the feel of it.

From a Hop the Fence

One way to describe this is that it feels similar to the Punching Bag. There are notable differences that we'll describe in the steps below.

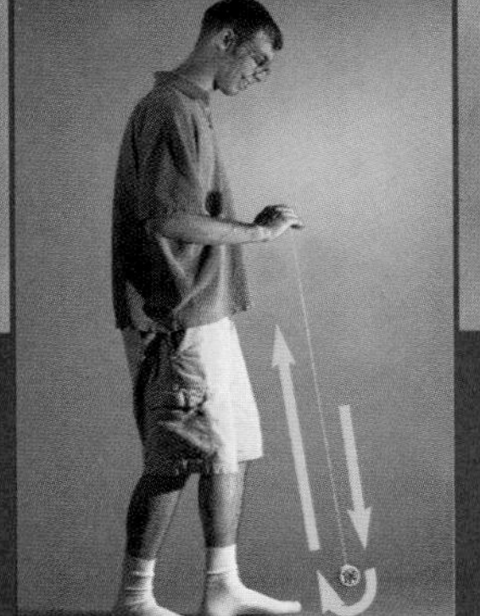
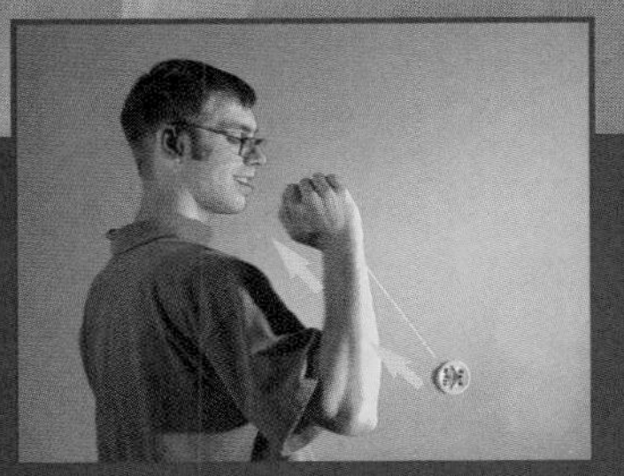

1. Start with a Gravity Pull. As the yo-yo comes back, guide it under your hand as you would for a Punching Bag. Instead of sending it straight out, however, you must cock your hand back and whip the yo-yo ...

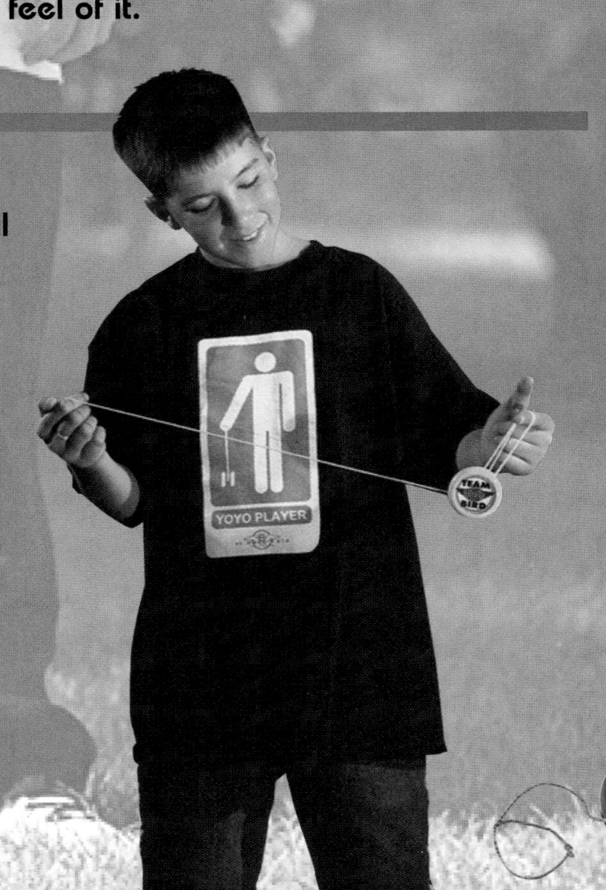

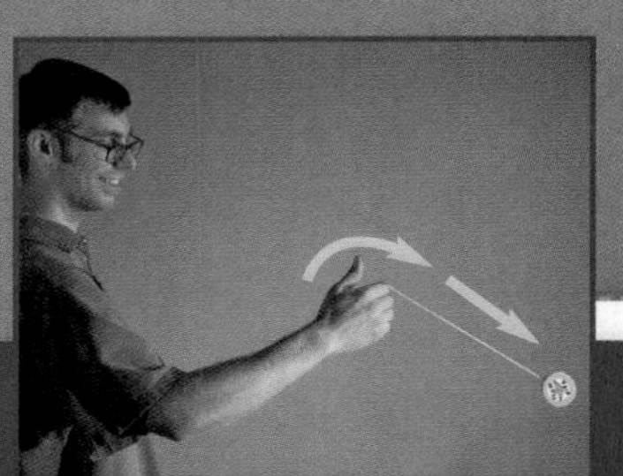

2. … down, as you would for a Hop the Fence. Your hand needs to guide this whole motion. The yo-yo will (if you threw it hard enough) get to the bottom spinning faster than when it came back from the Gravity Pull.

The hand motion is key in Regeneration. You control where the yo-yo goes and how fast it will spin when it gets there. The harder you whip your hand around, the faster the yo-yo will spin.

If your Loops and Hop the Fence are perfectly straight, then Regeneration probably won't give you any trouble. Most of us, however, will have to work hard to get the regenerated yo-yo to spin correctly.

You can use this technique from any trick that ends with a motion like the Forward Pass, Hop the Fence, or Sleeper. If we've said that a trick can end with a Loop, you can convert it into a Regeneration. Practice Regeneration of Spin a lot. It's very important to your continued development as a Spinner.

Like the tricks in this book, Regeneration of Spin is something you have to combine into your trick runs. The better you get at adding it in, the longer you can keep a run going. Imagine four minutes or more of yo-yoing without once catching the yo-yo. That's what you need Regeneration for.

Regeneration of Spin can make a series of unconnected tricks, each followed by a catch, into a smooth performance of a dozen tricks without stopping. The possibilities are staggering.

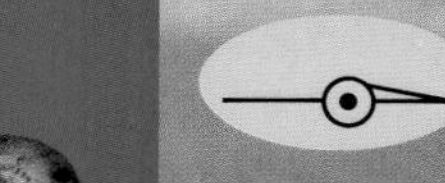

Triple Trapeze

This is a competition trick that tests your Regeneration abilities. It's essentially three Regenerated Man on the Flying Trapeze tricks, one right after the other. Take it from us—the Triple Trapeze is difficult.

1. Here you are in your first Man on the Flying Trapeze. Nothing too difficult about that one, is there?

2. Pop the yo-yo off the string and let it wind back toward your hand. Don't catch it!

3. Instead, whip it around your hand in a sideways Regeneration. The motion should be like a Hop the Fence, only the angle is different. Get ready to go into …

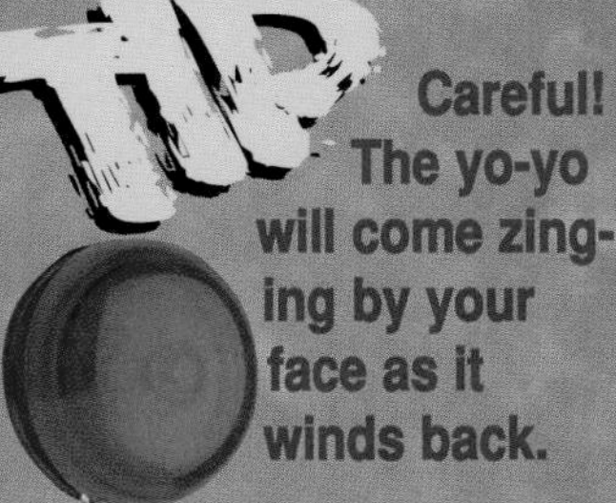

TIP Careful! The yo-yo will come zing-ing by your face as it winds back.

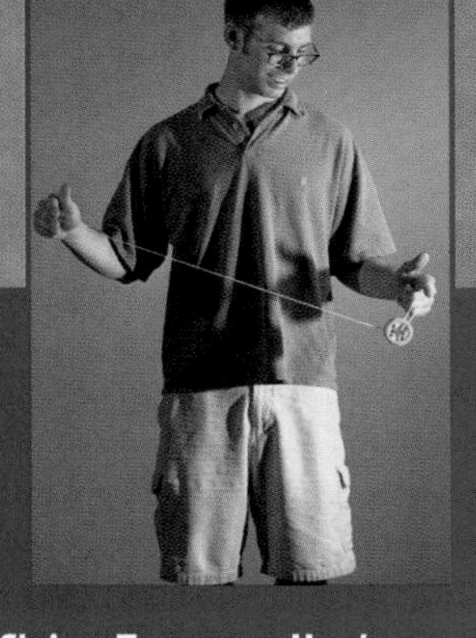

3. ... the second Man on the Flying Trapeze. You're doing really well if you've gotten this far. Now follow the first steps to get the third Trapeze and you're set!

Warp Drive

Batten down the hatches and get ready for a speedy trip. Warp Drive is three regenerated Around the Worlds. How do you regenerate Around the World? We'll show you.

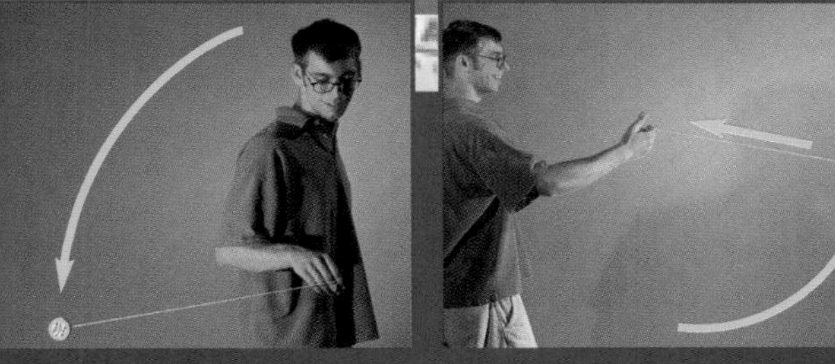

1. A good old Around the World. Once you complete one orbit, tug the yo-yo back toward your hand as though you were going to catch it. But don't.

Competition Tip

In competitions, the Warp Drive, as well as the Time Warp, usually must be *started* with a Loop that punches into the first Around the World.

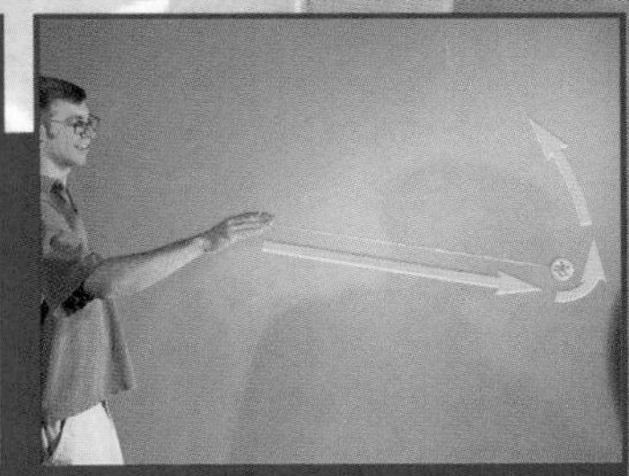

2. Instead, Loop the yo-yo hard over your hand. This will regenerate the spin and let you ...

3. ... do another Around the World. Follow the steps for the first one and you'll be blasting off at light speed.

Time Warp

What happens when you hit light speed? Some say you go back in time. Try this trick and see. It's two regenerated Around the Worlds punched into a Retro Around the World.

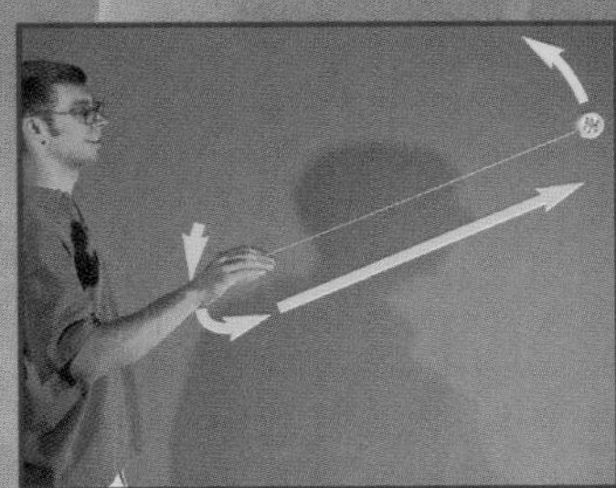

1. We're not showing this, but *start with a Loop*! This will get the Regeneration spin going and send you into the first Around the World.

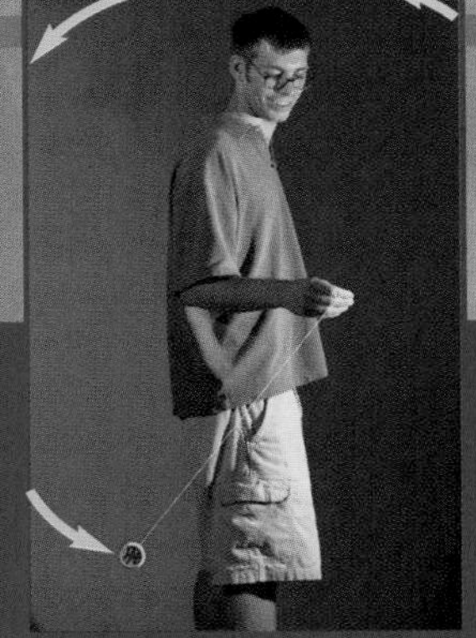

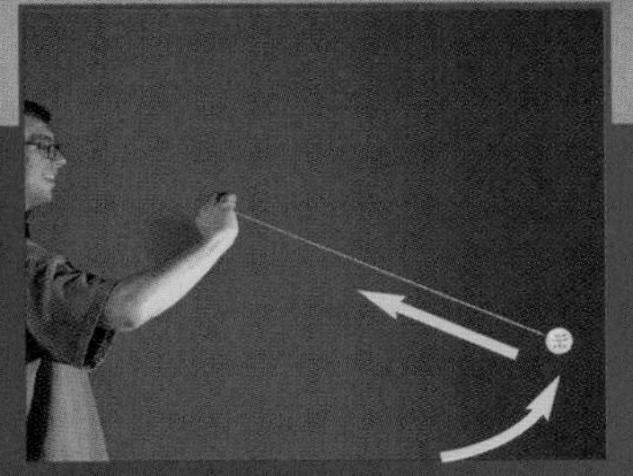

2. Do one orbit and then pull the yo-yo in for a Loop. Use the Loop to Regenerate the spin and off you go

3. When you've finished the second orbit, tug the yo-yo back. This time, you should guide the yo-yo *under* your hand and then back out. Use your Punching Bag motion. This will regenerate the yo-yo and send it off ...

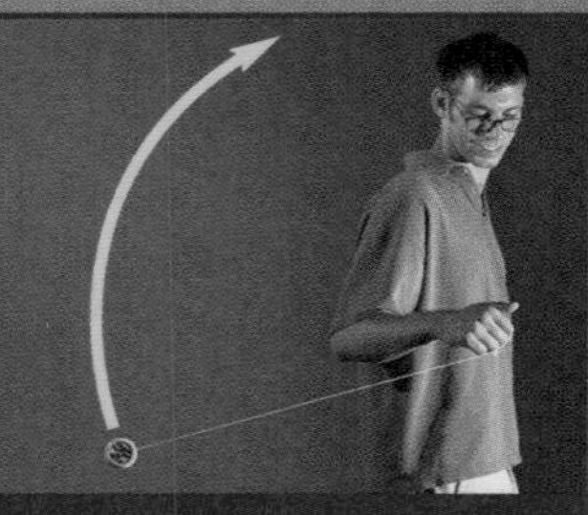

4. ... into a Retro Around the World. Let the yo-yo orbit and then call it back after an exhausting journey.

Moving On

Well, here you are at the end of all our one-handed tricks and Building Blocks. You've come a long, long way. You should be linking the moves together by now. Experiment with tricks to see which ones go together. Some of them fit like puzzle pieces.

The tricks in this book are by no means the only tricks in the world. You'll find them in the unlikeliest of places. Sometimes a new trick will pop up from the mess you made of an old trick.

Did any of you notice that we said *one*-handed tricks?

Look ahead and you'll see that we've included a section on the ultimate yo-yo challenge: Two-Handed Tricks.

You think Regeneration of Spin was tough? Wait until you get to Ride the Horse. Don't worry, though, we've got pictures and descriptions. And believe us when we tell you that you already know all the parts that make up two-handed tricks.

Before you go on, pat yourself on the back. These tricks you know now are not easy. You've done a lot of work to get here, and we say "Bravo!"

Now get that second yo-yo out and we'll see what you're made of ...

Two-Handed Tricks

So You Wanna Yo With Both Hands?

You say you can't even use a paper clip with your off hand? We say you can learn to yo with both hands. You can (especially if you've learned all the other tricks in this book) use two yo-yos, simultaneously, and convince people you're ambidextrous.

How?

How else? Practice, practice, practice.

Warming Up

The Off Hand

For righties, it's your left hand. For lefties, it's your right hand. For most of us, it's the hand we don't do too much with. It's usually weaker, less coordinated, and the place where we keep a wrist watch.

We're about to change all that. (Except for the watch bit. You can keep your watch.)

Take your yo-yo off your normal yo-yo hand. Transfer it over to your off hand and get ready! To be able to do two-handed tricks, you need to know how to do the following tricks with your off hand:

- Loop
- Outside Loop (we'll explain later)
- Hop the Fence
- Punching Bag
- Vertical Loops
- Reach for the Moon
- Around the World
- Retro Around the World
- Texas Cowboy

Once you've got all those down, it will be time to pull out a second yo-yo. Strap it onto your other hand and you'll be ready to try some simultaneous tricks. Let's rev it up and move 'em out.

TIP It's a good idea to have two yo-yos of the same type for two-handed tricks. That way you can get your hands into the same rhythm.

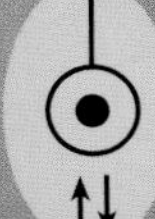

Gravity Pulls

Now is a good time to test your two-handed ability. Do a Gravity Pull with each yo-yo at the same time.

Did you make it? Try again. And again, and again. Keep going until it feels good and natural.

Now do alternating Gravity Pulls. Throw a Gravity Pull with one hand. When that first yo-yo hits the bottom of the string, throw the other yo-yo. Don't let the yo-yos sleep at the bottom.

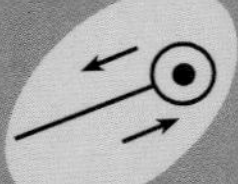

Forward Passes

Now that you have the feel of up-and-down motion with two yo-yos, let's try out and back.

Throw the two yo-yos out in a Forward Pass and then catch them as they come back.

Again. Out and back.

As with the Gravity Pulls, try alternating the Passes. One hand and then the other. Get the feeling into your muscle memory. When it doesn't feel awkward anymore, you're ready for the more difficult stuff. Read on!

Competition Tip

Try to complete five repetitions of each of these tricks. That's the *minimum* we want you to be able to do. Work your way up to 15 repetitions for each of them and you'll be confident of your ability. That confidence will make you much more likely to perform well at competitions.

Two-Handed Tricks

You're ready now. Your off hand is up to speed and you've got two yo-yos. Now all you need are some tricks! The descriptions below are spare and to the point. You already know the components of each of them; now you just have to combine them.

So go to it!

Loops

You can do Loops with each hand by itself. Now do them with both hands at the same time! Remember to keep your hands and arms steady, using your wrist to guide the action.

1. Loops with two hands. What could be easier?

Crisscross Loops

This is one looks complicated. You must Loop each yo-yo *across* your body. To keep the yo-yos from getting tangled, you must alternate your throws. Toss one yo-yo and then, when it is almost back in, toss the other. Think of it as if you are "marching" your throws: left hand, right hand, left hand, right hand.

1. Remember that you're still doing Loops. Keep those wrists going.

Milk the Cow

Back on the farm, there's chores that need a-doin'. Milk the Cow is when you do Hop the Fence with two hands. Keep those hands steady to keep the yo-yos under control.

1. Nothing too fancy about this one. Down, up, over, and down again.

Cattle Crossing

This here is just like Milk the Cow. Hop the Fence with two hands. Except this time, you crisscross them in front of you. Follow the tips in Crisscross Loops, one hand at a time, and you should be fine.

1. See? Keep those yo-yos alternating or you'll get tangled up.

Behind-the-Back Cattle Crossing

Who guessed? That's right! This trick is Cattle Crossing *behind* your back.

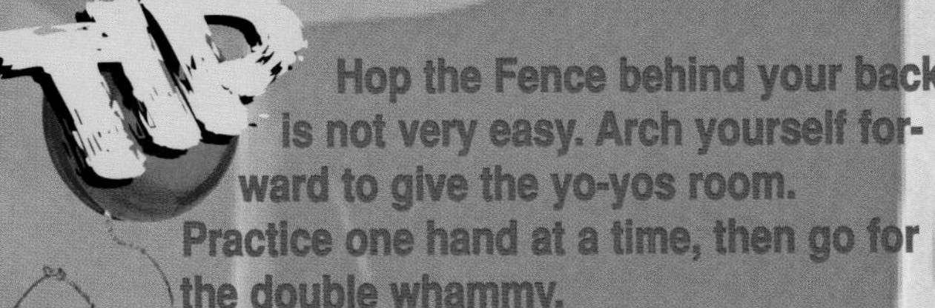

TIP Hop the Fence behind your back is not very easy. Arch yourself forward to give the yo-yos room. Practice one hand at a time, then go for the double whammy.

1. Notice how the hands are positioned. This position will let you do the trick without whacking yourself in the back.

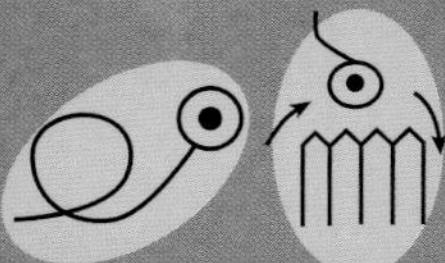

Ride the Horse

Here's another first for you. Your hands must do *different* tricks at the same time. One hand needs to Loop while the other does Hop the Fence *behind* you. Ride 'em cowboy!

1. Bounce while you Ride the Horse and it will look like you're … riding a horse.

TIP Just about all of the two-handed tricks are Loop types (Loops, Hop the Fence, Punching Bag, etc.). Remember that these will tighten and/or loosen your strings. Use your UFO throws to balance them out every now and then.

Loops & Punching Bag

Carrying on with the theme of each hand doing a different trick, we come to Loops & Punching Bag. Just as it sounds, one hand does Loops while the other does Punching Bag. This can be confusing. One yo-yo is looping under your hand and out again while the other is hopping over your hand and out. You choose which hand does which trick.

1. Seems easy enough in pictures, right? Try it out and see.

Two-Handed Punching Bag

You knew it would come to this, didn't you? Punching Bag with both hands. Remember to keep your hands steady; don't let them go higher and higher.

1. Work the bags like a pro. Float like a butterfly, sting like a bee.

Loops & Shoot the Moon

Another trick with major hang time. Don't force the Shoot the Moon. Take it nice and easy, just as if you were doing it with one hand.

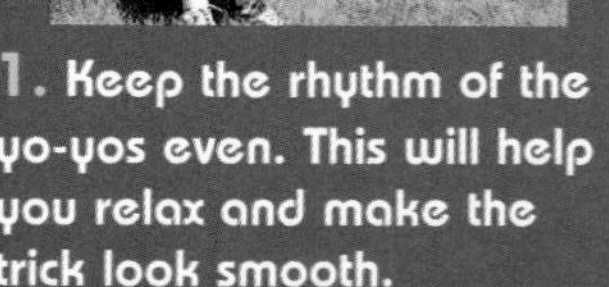

1. Keep the rhythm of the yo-yos even. This will help you relax and make the trick look smooth.

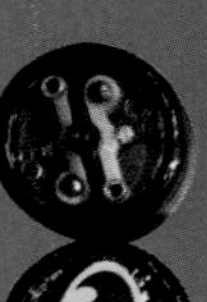

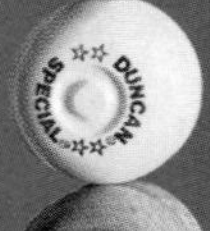

Two-Handed Vertical Loops

You know Vertical Loops. Now do them with both hands at once. Ta-da! Two-Handed Vertical Loops!

1. There they are. Up, up, and away.

Trivi-Yo

In 1985 a yo-yo was brought into space for the first time. It didn't work very well. Gravity is needed to get a yo-yo to do its stuff.

Shoot the Moon

Simply put, Shoot the Moon is Reach for the Moon with both hands. Like its one-handed cousin, Shoot the Moon should be graceful and smooth.

1. Don't try to huck the yo-yos up. Smooth wrist motions will get them up there.

Loops on Your Back

Not a very fancy name, but it lets you know what's expected. The best way to start this is standing up. Start doing your two-handed Loops. Bend your knees and squat down, then sit, then roll onto your back—all the while keeping the Loops going.

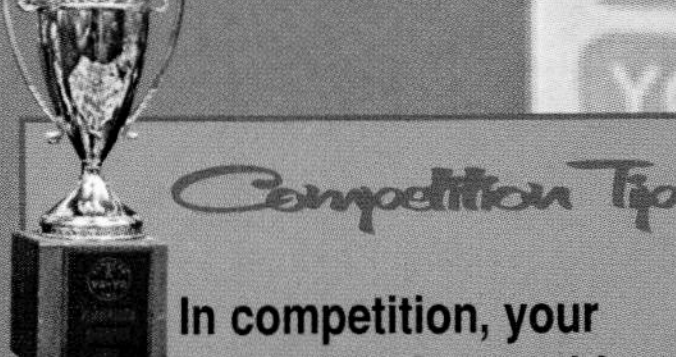

Competition Tip

In competition, your head *must* be touching the floor for your trick to count as Loops on Your Back. So stay low and flat.

Loops & Loops Under a Leg

No guessing here. One hand does Loops and the other hand does Loops under your leg. It's easiest to start doing the normal two-handed Loops and then, as one of the yo-yos is coming back in, lift your leg and send the yo-yo back out underneath it.

1. Make sure you have good balance so you can stay up there on one leg!

Loops & Loops Behind the Back

What do you suppose the name could mean? Loops Behind the Back is a new position for an old trick. It's awkward, but essentially the same as regular Loops.

Competition Tip
Try for three World Tours while continuing to Loop.

1. Here's a clear view of Loops Behind the Back. Keep them going while you do normal Loops with the other hand. Simple, no?

Sword & Shield

Here's a new twist. One hand does Loops while the other does a World Tour. At first, it may seem like the strings will tangle. And, on your first try, they just might. The secret is all in the timing.

1. The best advice is this: don't cross your strings! Seriously, time it so that the Loop is coming back in as the World Tour passes across the Loop path.

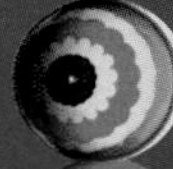

Helicopter

This chopper includes Loops that you do with one hand while doing an Around the World over your head! Remember the Texas Cowboy? This uses the same motion for the over-the-head throw.

1. When you bring the top yo-yo down, be careful of the looping yo-yo. You don't want to get caught in the 'copter blades.

Around the World (With Crisscross Variations)

Need we say more? Do Around the World with both hands. We'll illustrate a few variations on this here.

1. Here's the normal one. Make three or more orbits before calling your yo-yos back.

2. Now try the Crisscross Around the World variation two ways. This variation is with your hands alternating. They switch sides at the same time. Be careful not to cross the strings.

3. You can also Crisscross Around the World with your hands following one another from one side to the other. In this version, your hands are always on the same side. Separate them right before you return the yo-yos to your hands.

Loops & Crisscross Around the World

We're now back to Loops! One hand should continue looping while the other does the Crisscross Around the World. The orbit of the Around the World should keep the strings from crossing; just remember to move from one side to the other when the Around the World yo-yo is up above your Loop hand.

1. Notice that the Around the World hand goes *over* the Loop hand. This is extremely important if you're going to keep the strings free.

Two-Handed Warp Drive/ Time Warp

One hand should do three Around the Worlds. The other hand should do two Around the Worlds and then punch the yo-yo into a Retro Around the World.

1. They start out the same way, but after the Retro, the yo-yos are traveling in opposite directions.

Dale Oliver's "Moguls"

This is like Cattle Crossing. In this trick, however, you have one hand in front and the other behind your back. *Then* you start alternating back to front with each hand. Looks like you're skiing on moguls!

1. Start like this.

2. Start to switch your hands as the yo-yos come up. Bring the front to the back and the back to the front.

Retreat! (Reverse Sword & Shield)

The opposite of Sword & Shield. Do a Hop the Fence straight back with one hand and do a World Tour *behind* you. Tricky but funny when you do it right after a Sword & Shield charge. Look scared and shout "Retreat!" or "Run Away!"

1. Notice that the timing is important. This is very slippery because you can't see what's going on back there.

Whirlybird

This is also known as Whirlwind. It's a whole bunch of Inside-Outside Loops. This is one of the only times you'll do an Outside Loop. Your normal Loop travels inside the arm (we discussed this *way* back). An Outside Loop travels outside your arm (surprise!). Alternate between Inside and Outside Loops, and you've caught a Whirlybird.

1. One yo-yo is on the outside track, one is on the inside track. When they come back, send them out ...

2. ... on the opposite tracks! Also, you can alternate so that one yo-yo is going on the inside track while the other is going on the outside.

Wrist Crosses

These are tricky. You have to Loop with both hands and then start crossing your wrists. Right over left, then left over right, and back again. You'll suffer lots of bonks on the hands practicing this one.

1. Here are the wrists crossed.

2. And crossed the other way. The trick is in the timing, as usual, and you should do only *one* Loop while switching wrists. It's a faster action than you might think.

Moving on

More? You want more? Um ...

Well, let's wrap up, shall we?

This book, large as it is, only scratches the surface of the yo-yo tricks that are out there. If you count all the variations in standard tricks (a few more Barrel Rolls here, an Undercut there), there are literally *thousands* of them.

We hope that with the Building Blocks under your belt you'll be able to come up with variations of your own. Talk with your friends, go to contests, practice for hours, and you'll be surprised with what you can come up with.

We know that not all of you will know each and every trick in this book. That's fine. Keep practicing and working. If you know 50 percent of them, you're good. If you know 75 percent, you're golden.

No matter how many tricks you've mastered, though, when you feel strong in your yo handling and confident of your abilities, then it's time to check out ... contests!

Take that leap into the public and compete! In the next section, we have some tips and advice on how to find contests and what to do when you get there. Heed our words and you'll be up on stage in no time!

Yo-Yo Competitions

Where Do You Go from Here?

So you've mastered most of the tricks we've shown you. A few sketchy ones, but for the most part you don't even need to look at the pictures to get them right.

What's next?

How do you stack up against the other Spinners in your neighborhood? Your town? Your county, state, or the nation—even the world?

What you have to do now is enter a contest and pit your skills against those of other Spinners. You have to show up to a contest confident and prepared in order to do well, as in anything in life. In this section we have some information on what a contest will be like and what to expect. After all, entering a contest is one of the best ways to show the world what you have learned!

Competing is scary, but we'll try to prepare you the best we can. There's a lot for you to read, but if you know what you're getting into, you'll be more comfortable, less nervous, and more likely to have an edge on your competition.

The Bare Bones

Yo-yo contests have been described as similar to figure-skating competitions. Except there's no ice. And no skates. The costumes are less flashy. Oh, and there aren't any Zambonis involved.

However, as in a figure-skating competition, every competitor has a set of compulsory, or required, elements that are graded by judges.

That means that you will be given a list of tricks that you must perform. Successful completion of a trick earns points. Those Spinners with the highest point totals after the first round advance to a final round of more difficult tricks where a winner will be decided.

In larger contests with elite-level competitors, a "freestyle" element is added for those competitors making the final cut. The freestyle element is one of the most exciting parts of a contest. It's the part in which each Spinner has the chance to show off the best tricks in his or her arsenal, set to three minutes of music. The freestyle portion doesn't have to include a certain list of tricks, but the more tricks you do, the more points you get.

That's the basic format of a yo-yo contest. Now for some details.

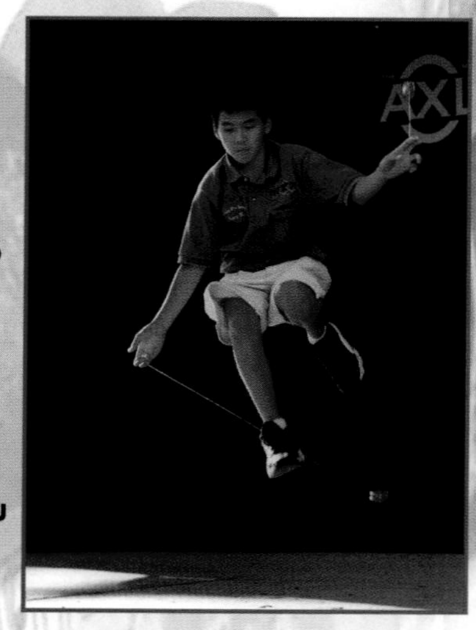

Divisions

Most contests have a few different divisions: Novice/Beginners, Advanced, Expert, National A (Single Handed), and National AA (Two Handed).

The Novice and Advanced divisions each have different age categories. For example, the 1998 U.S. Nationals included Novice Junior Youth for Spinners 10 years old and under and Novice Senior Youth for Spinners 11 to 15 years old.

Which one should you enter? The age question is easy but are you Novice or Advanced?

Here's where preparation comes in. Every contest should have a trick list available for you before the contest takes place. Study it!

This will give you, and the other competitors, a chance to hone your skills on the compulsory tricks and possible tiebreakers. The competition will have lists for each level, so enter the level that most suits your playing ability.

The Trick Square

All good contests are now using what is known as a trick square. This is a square measuring three feet by three feet in which any throw made by the player counts as an attempt. Be careful here. When we say any throw, we mean *any* throw. This includes just doing a Gravity Pull to make sure the string is wound correctly.

Step into the square only when you are ready to do the trick, the whole trick, and *nothing* but the trick. Then step back out once you've completed the trick.

Remember that while you're in front of the judges, you are always being judged. Do *not* practice the tricks while you are competing, even when you're outside the square. The judges will count any practicing of a trick as a *missed* attempt.

The only things you should do while being judged when you've stepped outside of the square are string adjustment tricks, such as Gravity Pull, *one* Loop, and UFO (unless this will be a trick). Check to see what the contest allows because what's allowed may vary from contest to contest.

You may do each of these string adjustment tricks multiple times if you throw *once and catch.* Be sure you are outside the square whenever you attempt them.

Show up prepared. Have your yo-yos tuned up (see "Care and Feeding") and bring plenty of string, finger protection, a glove, etc. Always have at least one or two extra yo-yos of the same model, tuned up exactly the same, in your pocket. Carry three or four for two-handed sections.

The last thing you want in a contest is to get a knot and spend five minutes trying to get the knot out in front of everyone. Just pull the replacement out of your pocket and you're ready to go!

Judging

So you've got a division you think is appropriate for you, you've been practicing the tricks, and you've taped off a trick square to practice in.

When you get up on stage in front of the judge and step into the trick square, you'll have two attempts and *two attempts only* to do each trick.

If you do the trick perfectly on the first try, you'll be given five points and can move on to the next trick. Miss it and you'll be given a second chance.

The second chance is worth only three points if you complete it successfully. Miss the trick a second time, and you get zero points and will be asked to move on to the next trick.

Sorry, no more than two attempts.

You'll have to do the tricks in the order in which the judges request them, which should be the same order in which they are listed in the trick lists for each division.

Judging a contest is a tough job. As you may have noticed, some of the tricks that we have listed in the book have more than one name. Also, there are different versions of some tricks, depending on whom you talk to. For example, perhaps what you know as a Texas Cowboy is known as a Whirlybird in a different state.

Competition Tip

You are *on stage.* Confidence and consistency count. Mentally prepare to be in front of hundreds, even thousands, of people while your every move is being scrutinized by the judges. This may seem scary, but if you know your tricks, you'll be fine.

Before the start of each division, the judges should always have someone demonstrate the tricks exactly as they are expected to be done. Pay *very* close attention when this is happening because you cannot practice the trick once the judging has begun. Don't even ask "Is this correct?" and try the trick. That will also be counted as an attempt.

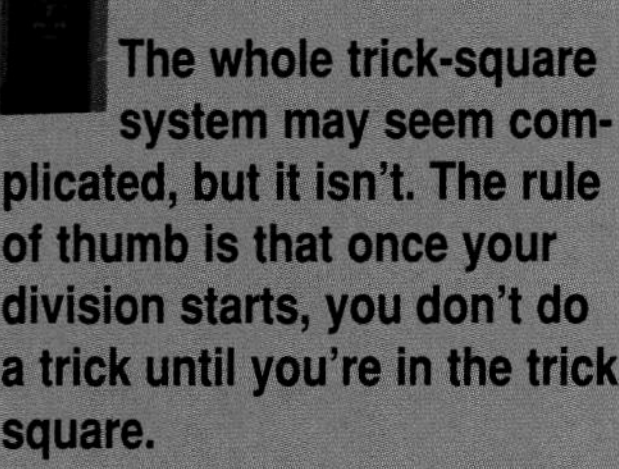

Competition Tip

The whole trick-square system may seem complicated, but it isn't. The rule of thumb is that once your division starts, you don't do a trick until you're in the trick square.

Freestyle

When you reach the pinnacle of yo-yo skill, you will need to enter a division that requires a freestyle routine. This is the most dynamic and fun part of a yo-yo contest. You have three minutes, set to music of your choice. Don't go over. Don't go under, either. Use all your time.

Showmanship plays a big part in freestyle. Work with your music and use your flashy moves. Remember to have a couple of spare yo-yos in your pockets.

Watch the Freestyle section of contests you attend, even if you're not participating. You'll get a feel for what is expected and what others have put together. These performances can be very impressive. Many never-before-seen tricks are debuted during the freestyle competitions.

Competition Tip

Sometimes the freestyle section is a separate division that can be entered by itself. Usually it's a part of the upper divisions. Make sure to always watch the freestyle competition. You'll usually see some amazing things!

Sample Trick Lists

Below are the full trick lists from two competitions. You can also find out about upcoming events and contests (as well as gathering other great yo-yo information) at these Web sites:

- **http://www.ayya.pd.net**—The American Yo-Yo Association. Lots of information and a good listing of events and contests.
- **http://www.nationalyoyo.org**—National Yo-Yo Museum Web site. Information about the U.S. National Championships, held the first Saturday in October every year.

The 1998 U.S. Nationals

National A—Single Handed

No age divisions

Compulsory One-Hand Element

- Creeper (full floor contact)
- Pinwheel (over fingers—three spins)
- Brain Twister (two somersaults)
- Hop the Fence (ten repetitions)
- 3 Leaf Clover (straight)
- Reach for the Moon (five repetitions)
- Trapeze, Two Somersaults (no flipovers)
- Double or Nothing (no flipovers)
- Warp Drive (three regenerated Around the Worlds)

- Loop the Loop (twenty-five Inside Loops)
- Split the Atom (split entry—two pass under—left and right —Somersault)
- Triple Trapeze (three regenerated Trapezes)
- Time Warp (forward World, regenerated backward World)
- Dizzy Baby (three over-the-top Pinwheels)
- Triple or Nothing (no flipovers)
- Texas Cowboy (jump over string)

Three-Minute Freestyle Element

Tiebreaker: Judge's Choice of Tricks

National AA—Two Handed

National Championship

No age divisions

Compulsory One-Hand Element

- Hop the Fence (ten repetitions)
- Reach for the Moon (ten repetitions)
- Brain Twister (two Somersaults)
- Split the Atom (split entry—two pass under—left and right—Somersault)
- Trapeze (one forward, one backward Somersault, no flipovers)
- Triple or Nothing (no flipovers)
- Warp Drive (three regenerated Worlds)
- Time Warp (forward World, regenerated backward World)

Compulsory Two-Hand Element

- Loop the Loop (ten repetitions)
- Crisscross (ten repetitions)
- Milk the Cow (ten repetitions)
- Ride the Horse (ten repetitions)
- Whirlwind (five Inside/Outside Loops)
- Reach for the Moon/Loop (five repetitions)
- Punching Bag (five repetitions)
- Shoot the Moon (five repetitions)

Three-Minute Freestyle Element

Tiebreaker: Judge's Choice of Tricks

Trivi-Yo

Pedro Flores, an immigrant from the Philippines, started making yo-yos in America. Flores sold the rights to a man named Duncan in 1929. The Duncan Yo-Yo was born. Flores was hired by Duncan to demonstrate the toy all over the country.

SCORING

Compulsory Elements—First try scores five points, second try scores three points.

Freestyle Element—Judging is based on the attempted difficulty, execution of routine, and showmanship.

Multiple judges will be used in scoring performance.

Novice

Junior Youth—10 Years Old and Under
Senior Youth—11 to 15 Years Old

- Gravity Pull
- Forward Pass
- Sleeper
- Break Away
- Walk the Dog
- Rock the Baby
- Around the World
- Loop the Loop

Recreational

Senior Youth—15 Years Old and Under
Old Folks—16 Years Old and Older

- Walk the Dog
- Creeper (advanced)
- Around the Corner (fingers must touch string)
- Tidal Wave (Skin the Cat) (draw string over fingers)
- Rock the Baby (three full rocks)
- UFO (pickup string)
- Hop the Fence (five repetitions)
- 3 Leaf Clover (last Loop straight down)
- Loop the Loop (five Inside Loops)
- Man on the Flying Trapeze (flipovers OK)

Tiebreakers:

- Brain Twister
- Trapeze with one Somersault
- Double or Nothing
- Judge's choice of tricks

Contest Rules and Guidelines

- Five inches of string outside the yo-yo is a miss.
- Practice throws allowed: Gravity Pull, Forward Pass, Loop, and string adjusts.
- A throw in the trick circle is an attempt.
- Only one yo-yo of any brand, transaxle or fixed axle, may be used.
- Judge's decision is final.

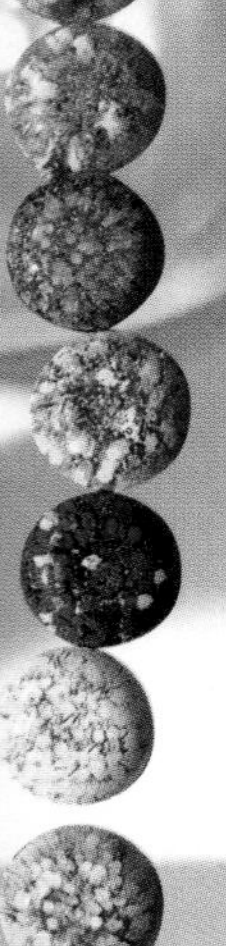

The 1999 Bay Area Classic

Novice

10 Years Old and Under

11 Years Old and Over

- Walk the Dog
- Creeper
- Around the World
- Hop the Fence (five times)
- Loop the Loop (three times)
- Around the Corner
- Rocket (the yo-yo must go one foot over the head)

Tiebreaker—Loop-Off

Advanced

16 Years Old and Under

17 Years Old and Over

- Creeper (walk out)
- Planet Hop (ten times)
- Dizzy Baby
- Texas Cowboy
- Brain Twister (one Somersault)
- Man on the Flying Trapeze (flipover OK)
- Shoot the Moon (three times)
- Loop the Loop (fifteen times)
- Pinwheel (pull-over, three spins)
- Barrel Rolls (three rolls)

Tiebreaker—Shoot the Moon (most repetitions win)

Masters—All Ages

- Shoot the Moon (ten times)
- Brain Twister (bottom Mount, two Front Somersaults with Loop ending)
- Punching Bag (ten times)
- Double or Nothing (Roll Out Dismount)
- Split the Atom (split entry—two pass under, left and right Loop ending)
- Triple or Nothing
- Warp Drive (start with Loop, three Around the Worlds)
- Vertical Loops (ten times)—these are Punching Bag Loops above your head
- Triple Trapeze
- Behind-the-Back Trapeze

Tiebreaker

Two-handed tricks:

- Two-Handed Loops (five times)
- Milk the cow (five times)
- Loop/Shoot the Moon (five times)
- Loop/Punching Bag (five times)
- Inside/Outside Loops (five times)

In case of another tie, the same two-handed trick will be done, but with ten repetitions.

Pro-Am Division—All Ages

All of these are also two-handed tricks.

- Wrist Crosses (five times)—left over right, right over left. One set of these will count as one repetition(no more than one Inside Loop allowed in between Crossover transitions).
- Double Vertical Loops (Ten times. These are two-handed Punching Bags above the head.)
- Cow Jumping Over the Moon (Ten times. Hop the Fence with one hand, Shoot the Moon with the other.)
- Lay-on-Back Loops (ten times with head on floor)
- Two-Hand Shoot the Moon (ten times)
- Behind-the-Back Cattle Crossing (five times)
- Two-Hand Warp Drive (Both hands doing Warp Drive on first two repetitions. On the last repetition, one hand doing Warp Drive, the opposite hand doing Time Warp.)
- Cattle Crossing (ten times)
- Two-Handed Punching Bags (ten times)
- Whirlwind (ten times)

Tiebreaker

In the event of a tie, these tricks will be sudden death/ one attempt only:

- Lay-on-Back Loops (fifteen times)
- Cattle Crossing (fifteen times)
- Two-Hand Shoot the Moon (fifteen times)

If there is still a tie, these tricks will be repeated.

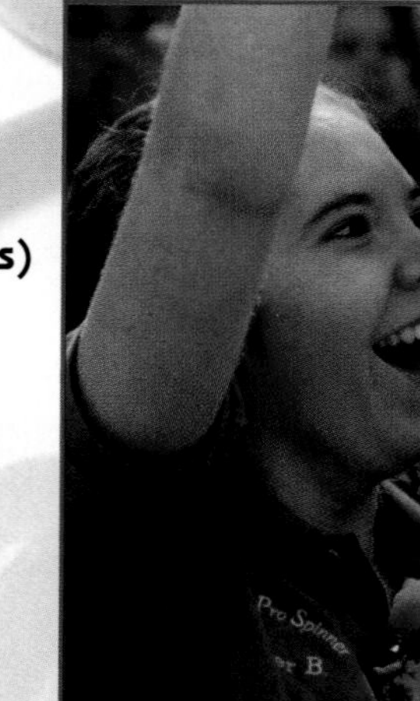

Wrapping it Up, Recapping

You're ready, you're set. So, here's a quick and easy list of things you should remember in competitions and a few new suggestions for your spinning pleasure. There's a whole wide world of yo-yos out there. Have at it!

- Two attempts at each trick. First try, five points; second try, three points. Two misses, zero points.
- The trick square is three feet by three feet, usually taped onto the stage. *Any* throw in the trick square counts as an attempt.
- Always make sure that you step into the square for the trick, then step back out when you've completed it.
- Judges will demonstrate the tricks at the beginning of each division. This is *exactly* how the trick is supposed to be done for the contest. Pay close attention.
- Know the trick list as far in advance of the contest as possible.
- Don't sandbag to a lower division than the one at which you are capable of performing. This is frowned on by judges and other players.
- Find out when registration is and get there early! Know when your division starts and get there early!
- Freestyle is three minutes of your best stuff set to music—the three-minute mark is exact and timed. Don't go over. Don't go under.
- Try putting together your own neighborhood, school, club, or city contest. Feel free to include fun events like longest Dragster races, longest Sleeper, highest Rocket, most Loops, and so on.
- Have fun! That's why you started using a yo-yo! Contests are a place to test your skills, meet other Spinners, and share tricks.

The National Yo-Yo Museum

Museums are usually still. Stuffed monuments stand in dusty silence while folks mill about quietly. The exhibits are so far removed from us in time that we can't begin to imagine how the subjects moved, how the objects were used.

Not here.

Not at the National Yo-Yo Museum in Chico.

The brightly painted woods and colorful plastics that fill the display racks and cases at this museum are all very familiar. We can hear the buzz of string against an axle, or the slap of the yo-yos in our palms. The shapes are ones we've played with and mastered, or broken, or set aside long ago. But each of us can remember when we learned, or tried to learn, how to yo.

"When you talk about yo-yos, you're really talking about peoples' childhoods," Bob Malowney says as he stands in the museum. Bob, with his wife Barbara, owns the store Bird in Hand. An entire corner of the store is given over to the National Yo-Yo Museum and a large rack is nearby to display the yo-yos for sale.

Bird in Hand has sponsored the National Yo-Yo Tournament for 11 years now. One of the coveted titles in the yo-yo world is the National Champ, decided each year in Chico.

All that is months away, however, as Bob points out to us five display cases along the wall. Each one is full, top to bottom, with yo-yos. Each one represents a different decade, from the '50s to the '90s.

"People can find themselves on this timeline by finding the yo-yos they had when they were kids," he says.

Professional models, wooden ones, plastic, novelty, promotional. It seems that all of them are here.

A pair of boys stare at the '90s case while their parents point at different models in the '60s and '70s cases. Several display stands feature patches and booklets from the '50s, the most prolific yo-yo period until now. Bob points to the booklets. They show all the prizes kids could win in a competition. Everything from a jacket patch to a new beach-cruiser bicycle.

"Why were yo-yos so big in the '50s?" he asks. "Reward for achievement. You were given a winner's attitude if you competed."

Trivi-Yo

The world's largest *working* yo-yo is at the National Yo-Yo Museum. It weighs 256 pounds and was yo-ed from an 80-foot tall crane to set a world's record.

He points to examples of the prizes in the museum cases. "They gave you patches, a prized yo-yo, a certificate, or even just a pat on the back. That reward for achievement is not entirely lost in this period of resurgence."

The reward for achievement works well in Chico. Bird in Hand sponsors Team Bird, a group of kids you know well, having seen their pictures all over this book.

Team Bird is composed of local kids who want to learn how to yo. Thaddaeus Winzenz and Joe Arnold teach them on Saturdays at the store. As the kids get better, they can demonstrate their skills. If they can complete a certain set of tricks, they get a T-shirt. Another set wins them a hat. And so on.

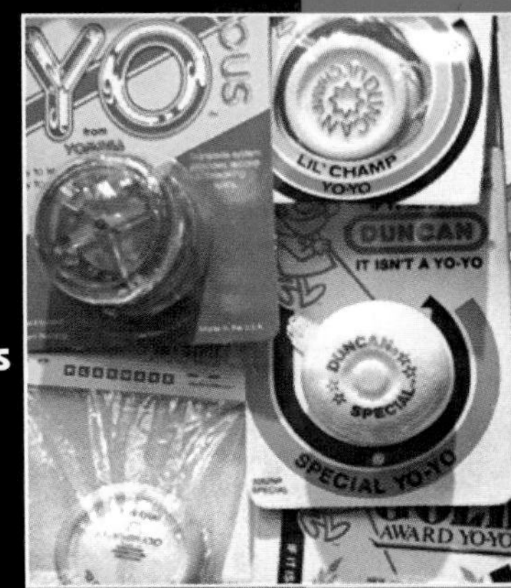

As the tricks get more difficult and the repetitions get longer, the prizes get better.

More important than the objects they win, however, is the attitude they gain. Team Bird members have all accomplished something. They've learned skills that most people would give up on. They've won.

The museum is a place to find your yo-yo. To once again revisit, or for the first time discover, a simple, engaging toy that fascinates generation after generation. Unlike most other museums, the National Yo-Yo Museum is a tribute to speed, accuracy, and energy—all the things that keep yo-yos in our culture.

Yo-yos have been here for many years, and they're back again in force. Bob Malowney, for one, is sure that they'll never disappear.

See and Be Seen

So you say you can do a Brain Twister? Prove it! Below you'll see a checklist of all the tricks in this book. After each trick name there are three lines for witness initials.

Here's what you do. Practice until you're confident enough to do the tricks in front of someone. Then, ask them to witness for you. Do your trick and then have the witness put his or her initials on the checklist if you complete the trick successfully.

You can have the same person witness all three times, or have three different people witness for you. However, if you do the trick *once* in front of *three* people, they don't get to initial all three lines.

This is good practice for competitions in that it makes you get up in front of someone and perform your tricks under pressure. Also, if you can do a trick successfully three times on three separate occasions, then you can be confident that you know the trick.

Practice your moves and go find a willing audience.

Good luck!

TIP Pretend it's a competition. If you mess up the trick on your first and second attempts, then your witness shouldn't initial the line. Practice some more and then try again later.

Checklist

Beginning Building Blocks

Trick	Witness 1	Witness 2	Witness 3
Gravity Pull	____	____	____
Sleeper	____	____	____
Forward Pass	____	____	____
Inside Loop	____	____	____
Break Away	____	____	____

Beginning Tricks

Trick	Witness 1	Witness 2	Witness 3
Walk the Dog	____	____	____
Walk the Cat	____	____	____
Dragster	____	____	____
Creeper	____	____	____
Around the World	____	____	____
World Tour	____	____	____
Rock the Baby	____	____	____
Rocket	____	____	____
Tidal Wave	____	____	____
Around the Corner	____	____	____
Elevator	____	____	____
Monkey on a String	____	____	____
Over the Falls	____	____	____
3 Leaf Clover	____	____	____
Hop the Fence	____	____	____
Planet Hop	____	____	____

Intermediate Building Blocks

Trick	Witness 1	Witness 2	Witness 3
Basic Front Mount	____	____	____
Roll Out Dismount	____	____	____
MOFT	____	____	____
Drop Dismount	____	____	____
Back Off Dismount	____	____	____
Fly Away	____	____	____

Intermediate Tricks

Trick	Witness 1	Witness 2	Witness 3
UFO	____	____	____
Restart	____	____	____
Front Pinwheel	____	____	____
Dog Bite and Pit Stop	____	____	____
Texas Cowboy	____	____	____
Dizzy Baby	____	____	____
Tiny Baby	____	____	____
Trapeze Baby	____	____	____
One-Handed Star	____	____	____
Eiffel Tower	____	____	____
Yo-Maneuver	____	____	____
Brain Twister	____	____	____
Quick Draw	____	____	____
30 Loops	____	____	____
10 Opposite-Hand Loops	____	____	____

Advanced Building Blocks

Trick	Witness 1	Witness 2	Witness 3
Front Mounts:			
Under Mount	___	___	___
Over-Under Mount	___	___	___
OU Mount Variations:			
From the Over Mount	___	___	___
From the Pinwheel	___	___	___
Shotgun	___	___	___
Roller Coaster Mount	___	___	___
Hydrogen Bomb Mount	___	___	___
Double or Nothing	___	___	___
Double or Nothing: Dismount	___	___	___
Triple or Nothing	___	___	___
Reverse Double or Nothing	___	___	___
Ferris Wheel Dismount	___	___	___
Lindy Loops	___	___	___
Barrel Rolls	___	___	___
Barrel Rolls: MOFT	___	___	___
Undercuts	___	___	___
Somersaults	___	___	___
Backflip	___	___	___

Advanced Tricks

Trick	Witness 1	Witness 2	Witness 3
Atom Bomb	___	___	___
Split the Atom: Basic	___	___	___
Split the Atom: Advanced	___	___	___
Hydrogen Bomb	___	___	___
Roller Coaster	___	___	___
Reach for the Moon	___	___	___
Magic	___	___	___
Drop in the Bucket	___	___	___
Punching Bag	___	___	___
Vertical Loops	___	___	___
Retro Around the World	___	___	___

Regeneration of Spin

Trick	Witness 1	Witness 2	Witness 3
From a Hop the Fence	___	___	___
Triple Trapeze	___	___	___
Warp Drive	___	___	___
Time Warp	___	___	___

Two-Handed Tricks

Trick	Witness 1	Witness 2	Witness 3
The Off Hand	___	___	___
Gravity Pulls	___	___	___
Forward Passes	___	___	___
Loops	___	___	___
Crisscross Loops	___	___	___
Milk the Cow	___	___	___
Cattle Crossing	___	___	___
Behind-the-Back Cattle Crossing	___	___	___
Ride the Horse	___	___	___
Loops & Punching Bag	___	___	___
Two-Handed Punching Bag	___	___	___
Loops and Shoot the Moon	___	___	___
Two-Handed Vertical Loops	___	___	___
Shoot the Moon	___	___	___
Loops on Your Back	___	___	___
Loops & Loops Under a Leg	___	___	___
Loops and Loops Behind the Back	___	___	___
Sword and Shield	___	___	___
Helicopter	___	___	___
Around the World (w/ Crisscross Var.)	___	___	___
Loops and Crisscross ATW	___	___	___
Two-Handed Warp Drive/Time Warp	___	___	___
Dale Oliver's Moguls	___	___	___
Retreat!	___	___	___
Whirly Bird	___	___	___
Wrist Crosses	___	___	___

Trick Directory

YoForIt.com is *the* place for all your yo-yo needs. Point your web browser over to the best yo-yo resource on the net—www.YoForIt.com!

www.YoForIt.com

Trick of the Week

Take a look at the super-cool trick section where the resident yo-yo pros demonstrate a new trick every week. With everything from beginning to advanced levels of tricks, you'll soon be spinning with the best of them.

Online Ordering

Can't find the yo-yo you're looking for? You could waste countless hours driving from place to place searching for the right yo-yo, or you could log on to YoForIt.com. YoForIt.com has expert reviews of all yo-yo models, so you can't make a bad decision. YoForIt.com is the place to go for all of your yo-yo needs.

Yo-Yo Giveaways!

There's only one thing better than a good yo-yo... a *free* yo-yo! Check out the Sweepstakes section of YoForIt.com for details on how to win cool stuff.

Ask Doc Yo!

Do you have a tough question about yo-yos that nobody seems to have the answer to? Forget climbing a mountain in Peru to find some guru, just ask Doc Yo.

When do I replace my ball bearing? How do I know when my string is about to snap? Do the lunar cycles really matter when I'm trying to "Split the Atom"?

You can find answers to all these questions and more on Ask Doc Yo. Doc Yo knows it all, and he's here to tell you. Just ask!

Contest Info

Show off your yo-yo Skills!

To find out the latest contest information, check out the event section of the web site. You will find dates; locations, and the list of tricks you need to compete in regional, national, and worldwide contests.

These events are a great place to learn more about the world of yo-yoing. Once there, you will meet new friends, pick up tricks from the experts, *and* have a whole lot of fun!